# The World of the Scythians

# The World of the Scythians

by Renate Rolle

Translated by F.G. Walls
from the German *Die Welt der Skythen*

University of California Press
Berkeley and Los Angeles

© 1980 Verlag C.J. Bucher
First published in German 1980
English translation University of California Press
First published in English 1989

Typeset by Lasertext Ltd, Manchester, England
and printed in Great Britain by
The Bath Press, Bath
Published by University of California Press
Berkeley and Los Angeles

ISBN 0-520-06864-5

# Contents

# Introduction

## 'They're Scythians!'

*'Quel effroyable spectacle! Ce sont eux-mêmes! Tant de palais! Quelle résolution extraordinaire! Quels hommes! Ce sont des Scythes!'*[1]

Thus exclaimed Napoleon in horror as he gazed through the red-hot windows of the Kremlin Palace at the conflagration which was steadily approaching. (The Russians are said to have set fire to their own capital city in order to force a French retreat.) General Ségur, to whom we owe the account of this scene in the Moscow of 1812, also describes the feelings of the French Emperor at that moment: 'Having struck at the heart of an empire, he was astonished to find that the reaction was not that of terror and submission. He felt that he had met a people with a resolve superior to his own and that he had been defeated.'

Napoleon was interested in archaeology, and the blazing inferno may have reminded him of Herodotus's account over two thousand years ago, in Book IV of the *Histories*, of the failure of the Persian King Darius's campaign against the Scythians. When threatened in 513/12 BC by Darius's huge army, raised especially to subjugate them, the Scythians developed a brilliant system of delaying tactics which eventually proved completely successful. Luring the Persians deep into their territory, they destroyed wells, burned food and trampled their own pastureland. In this way they sought to wear down the invaders, and through their superior horsemanship, according to ancient sources, the Scythians nearly brought about the total destruction of the Persian army. It may have occurred to Napoleon that day in Moscow that those events

were said to have taken place only a few hundred miles to the south, in the steppes of what is now the Ukraine. His horrified exclamation: 'They're Scythians!' refers in this context to a particular fighting strategy and mentality which was associated by writers of classical times with the Scythians, an association which has survived into the modern age.

If we look back to ancient sources, a fair amount can be gleaned about the Scythians from their neighbours. In the eyes of an Achaemenid Persian, the Scythians (or Sakas) were the people in the north who were constantly restless, exotically colourful and posed a perpetual threat. King Darius had succeeded in vanquishing the Asiatic Scythians in 520/19 BC, and their King, Skuka, was bound and led before him. The huge relief on the rock face of Bisutun, a massif on the road from Kermanshah to Hamadan in western Iran, shows a larger-than-life Darius and nine subjugated enemy kings. The last on the right is Skuka, King of the Sakas of the 'pointed helmets'. A multilingual inscription proclaims the Persian victory over him. By contrast the compaign against the European Scythians six years later, mentioned above, was a disaster. The Persian King was insulted and disgraced, and driven back to the Hellespont – and indeed almost further – together with his huge army. Only the systematic destruction of all aids to the crossing of the Scythian army prevented anything worse happening at that time, as we are told in Book XIII of Strabo. As might be expected, there is no Persian account of this ignominious defeat. The present-day visitor to Persepolis will encounter ancient representations of tribute-bearing Scythian or Sakan delegations who, in contrast to deputations from other peoples, are

7

always depicted carrying arms: certainly somewhat unusual for a 'tributary' people.

In the eyes of the classical Greeks the Scythians were northern barbarians with bizarre and bloodthirsty customs. One of the former was their habit of drinking wine neat, which horrified their contemporaries, giving rise to the Greek saying 'drinking the Scythian way', which meant 'getting blind drunk'. Owing to the constant traffic, these drinking, hemp-inhaling lords of the steppes north of the Hellespont, who loved pomp and show, had been well known at least since the fifth century BC, even in Athens, and they did anything but inspire confidence. They were, however, famed for being excellent warriors, and in ancient times thought to be invincible. At one with their horses and bows, they resembled centaurs, and the Greeks coined a new word, 'horse-archers', to describe them.

Schoolchildren are told of the Greeks' heroic battles against superior Persian forces. The Scythians, however, share the fate of all peoples who had no writing – what we know from written sources originates from foreign observers, often even from enemies, and is correspondingly tendentious.

Present-day historians and classical scholars derive their notion of the Scythians primarily from the colourful and tolerant description given by Herodotus (Book IV), whose travels took him to the southern border of Scythia. There is also an account by one of the authors of the Hippocratic treatise ('De aere, aquis, locis' in *Corpus Hippocraticum*), which gives the impression of being more factual.

There has, however, been far more scepticism about Herodotus's description than about the account of the pseudo-Hippocrates, which documents the view of the contemporary physician. Yet despite the latter's appearance of being scientific and precise, it is clearly more distorted than the former owing to the author's personal, aesthetic and cultural reactions and his intense aversion to riding and life on horseback and in waggons.

The present-day theatre-goer, interested in Greek comedies such as those of Aristophanes, will be familiar with the figure of the Scythian dressed for the most part in fantastic costume.

Recruited as keepers of law and order, Scythians had long been a frequent and everyday sight in Athens and were favourite objects of ridicule for the comic playwrights of the day – always drunken and licentious, and speaking broken Greek.

Similarly, most people today either have a false picture of the Scythians or the word means practically nothing to them, unless they happen to have seen the magnificent evidence of their culture in the museums of Leningrad, Moscow or Kiev. But even then, the actual 'land of the Scythians' remains closed to them, not least owing to the fixed tourist routes for foreigners.

Few archaeologists are familiar with Russian, the language in which almost all modern specialist literature is published. Only the finds from the frozen tombs of Pazyryk in the Altai have become more widely known, since much was also published about them in the West. Despite their richness they are however of only peripheral importance within Scythian culture and do not, in isolation, provide adequate grounds for assessment. A somewhat exaggerated parallel would be if we were to reconstruct the whole of Roman culture on the basis of finds from their military outposts in the rugged, misty region of Germania.

In the meantime several excellent finds from recent Soviet excavations have been made accessible to a wider public, through exhibitions in various countries in the West. 'Scythian gold' – and unfortunately in most cases only that – has thus become relatively well known. In an age obsessed with superlatives it is this gold alone which accounts for the renewed interest in the Scythians, which they deserve and which was indeed not lacking in earlier periods, even in scholarly German and English literature.

Literature on the Scythians is orientated towards popular science and dominated, with few exceptions, by stereotyped views of the Scythians and their culture. This is due in large measure to the working methods of archaeologists, especially those in the last century. Excavation work was confined to graves of the Scythian ruling class, which were purposely sought because of the objects of precious metal which they contained. Their scientific investigation would often be rigorously curtailed if evidence of a grave-robbery was found, indicating that there would no longer be any gold to find. This attitude, together with the lack of interest in settlements or in the graves of the less privileged members of the populace, which naturally did not contain such beautiful and rich deposits, meant that the only available information concerned a minute proportion of Scythians. Even the Russian exile Michail Rostowzew, in his great work, *Skythien und der Bosphorus* (*Scythia and the Bosporus*, Berlin, 1931), does not in fact deal with the 'normal' Scythian, basing his archaeological sections almost exclusively on finds from the tombs of the rich and distinguished. Furthermore, there was no archaeological research into settlement. All this contributed to the view that Scythian culture comprised only the culture of a nomadic ruling class which enabled the 'lower' classes to lead idle lives of amusement as vagrant horse-breeders, and whose ideals centred on war and the acquiring of booty. Since there had long been no anthropological examination of the skeletons found, contradictory and false assumptions concerning the physical characteristics of the Scythians remained unchallenged. These culminated in the image of the Scythians as without exception small, bow-legged, fat creatures of an extreme Mongol type.

In addition, as a result of contemporary political events the Scythians became the butt of the most absurd prejudices. Their acquisition of land in the first millennium BC was seen as a threat to the civilization and culture of ancient Europe, and the present-day Iron Curtain is interpreted as the continuation of the former western boundary of the Scythian's sphere of control.

Ever since it first emerged from the obscurity of the burial chambers, Scythian art has attracted intense interest. A series of magnificent publications ensured that many of the exquisite finds were made available to a fairly wide public.[2]

In the meantime, new excavations and research in the Soviet Union and immediate neighbouring areas has completely transformed the image of the Scythians. The most important findings, which compel us to re-examine and revise completely our ideas of ancient horse-riding nomadic cultures, will be dealt with in this book. The basic conditions for this new level of scientific knowledge consist first of all in the setting up of large-scale excavations together with archaeological settlement research. For the necessary shifting of earth, Soviet archaeologists made use of building machinery very early on – not least owing to pressure exerted by plans for technical projects such as canals and reservoirs etc. Bulldozers, scrapers and cranes are now the order of the day, and the archaeologist often has to wear a protective helmet while at work.

In the Soviet Union excavations and archaeological expeditions are generally the province of the central institutions of the Academy of Science in the main cities of the Soviet republics. The centre for modern research into the Scythians is Kiev. Finds are accumulating in the city museums, and the treasure chamber of the Kiev cave monastery of Lavra today contains one of the most impressive collections of Scythian gold. All precious-metal objects discovered in the Ukraine since 1917, which were not destroyed in the Second World War, are concentrated there.

As in other countries, archaeology in the Soviet Union is linked with a number of other, primarily scientific disciplines. Today this interdisciplinary work enables a new, different assessment of the level of economic development and potential of the Scythians, and of their practices in art and religion. Thousands of systematically excavated burial grounds already enable us to present evidence based on broad statistical findings. The graves of princes and kings – not only unearthed, but completely exposed and thoroughly documented – allow numerous deductions about the ruling classes and testify to their power over the possessions, labour and life of others even after death. The examination and evaluation of the many and varied objects of weaponry now enables us to make positive statements regarding the military equipment and fighting methods of the Scythians. They also show us the fundamentals of that Scythian fighting prowess which was so much feared in ancient times. Investigations in areas which in the seventh and sixth centuries BC were targets of nomadic equestrian military campaigns, and where vast tracts of destruction have been established, also make possible deductions about the fighting strategy of the invaders. The greatest and most astounding discoveries, however, must include the unearthing of large fortifications and 'urban' settlements.

All this has resulted in the transformation of an archaeological view which previously seemed unalterable. It is the intention of the present work to give an account of this process.

# 1  The land of the Scythians

## Reconstruction of the ancient topography

Ancient Scythia lay between the Danube in the west and the Don in the east. During certain phases of Scythian history, however, it extended far beyond this: thus Caucasia (the 'Scythian road') in the south-east, and Dobruja ('Scythia Minor') in the west, were included from time to time. The northern boundary cannot be established with any precision, and scholarly opinion is divided on the subject. The first view is that the northern boundary stretched along a line roughly coinciding with present-day Kiev; according to the second, it ran about 124 miles (200 km) to the south of this along a geographical dividing line which is still important today: that between the grass steppes of the south and the forest steppes of the north. The Black Sea formed Scythia's southern boundary, and the geographers of antiquity compared its shape to a drawn Scythian bow. The extreme ends of this 'bow' are bounded on both sides by straits, the Thracian Bosporus in the west and the Cimmerian Bosporus in the east.

To the Greeks the Black Sea was 'the most wonderful of all seas', with water sweeter than all the others. However, it was also notoriously dangerous, with its shallows, thick mists and extremely violent and unpredictable storms which smashed the ships against the towering cliffs of a coast which had very few natural harbours. Nevertheless, the Greeks gave the Black Sea the name *Pontos Euxenios* or 'hospitable sea'. In Roman times Ovid called it the 'Scythian Sea'.

Apart from the ancient name 'Scythia' and the plain geographical term 'north Black Sea area', present-day scholarly nomenclature also includes the terms 'northern Pontus area' and 'north Pontic steppes' (derived from the Greek) to describe the land of the Scythians. After the Russian colonization the terms 'South Russia' and 'New Russia' emerged, chiefly in the nineteenth century. From a modern political and geographical standpoint, the borders of classical Scythia roughly correspond to those of present-day central and southern Ukraine, although they extend beyond it, particularly in the east.

From south to north this area is divided topographically into volcanic Crimea, steppe plateau and adjoining forest steppes, and this last area merges into the forest zone proper just north of Kiev. In the east the steppe zone becomes the steppes of the Volga and Ural district, extending as far as Kazakhstan, the Altai, Tuva and Mongolia.

## The Siberia of the Greeks

From the sixth century BC, during the course of a fairly extensive wave of colonization, a considerable number of Greek settlements grew up on the narrow northern coastal strip of the Black Sea. According to ancient sources this migration started from the town of Miletus in Asia Minor, and we must assume that its success was due to good relations with the indigenous population.

The most important new foundations, which soon developed into towns, were *Olbia*, situated on the estuary of two large rivers, the Hypanis (present-day Bug) and the Borysthenes (Dnieper), *Tyras*, modern Belgorod-Dnestrovski, on the bank of the Dniester, and *Nymphaion* and *Chersonesos Taurica* in the

Crimea. A further group of settlements developed on the banks of the Cimmerian Bosporus, which the Greeks considered to be the boundary between Europe and Asia. Among these were *Panticapaeum* (modern Kerch) – still on the European side – which in the period following became the capital of the Bosporan empire; *Phanagoreia*, already on the Asian side; and *Tanais* in the Don delta, on the northeast tip of ancient Maeotis (Sea of Azov).

At that time the vast north Pontic area was settled by various ethnically distinct peoples, dominated by Scythian tribes: the Tauri in the southern Crimea, the Neuri in the north west, the Agathyrsi in the west, the Androphagi, Melanchlaeni and Geloni in the north, the Sauromatians in the east, and the Sindi and Maeotae in the south-east.

There are many documented instances which show that intermarrying between Greeks and Scythians, as well as other indigenous peoples, was not at all uncommon in

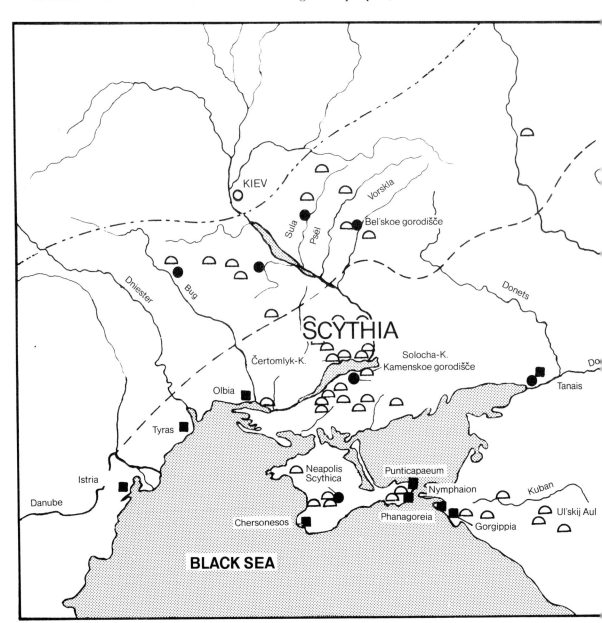

this area. The mother of Demosthenes, for example, was the child of such a union (from the north coast of the Black Sea). Demosthenes, as the grandson of a rich Scythian woman, was repeatedly accused by malicious opponents in Athens of being a barbarian who was merely availing himself of the Greek language.

Most of the towns founded by the Greeks experienced intense growth in the fifth century, acquiring substantial fortifications, extensive harbours, residential and temple districts, market-places and manufacturing centres etc. Many of these towns survived into the first centuries AD and were not destroyed until the time of the great migration. They are of particular significance for the period in question, as they maintained extensive trade relations with the peoples of the Pontic-Caspian steppes to the north, so that we are indebted to them for numerous written records. The terms *hippemolgi* and *galactophagi* ('horse-milkers' and 'milk-eaters') had already appeared in the works of classical writers, and since we know of these from later periods as synonyms for Scythians the descriptions – in Homer's *Iliad* (XIII, 1–7) for example – almost certainly refer to them. However a profound and – as later transpired – accurate knowledge of these peoples was first demonstrated by Greek merchants and travellers who were in direct contact with them. As already mentioned, the most important of these was Herodotus. In his Book IV, the impressions of his journey to Olbia and a wealth of notes, probably the result of numerous conversations with the inhabitants of the town who called themselves Olbiopolites or Borysthenites, are brought together in a fascinating description of country and people.

Herodotus seems to have been interested in this country because he wanted to visit and observe the scenes of certain events of which he had heard. In particular he was interested in the terrain of the Persian campaign against Scythia (513/12 BC). It is easy to explain why Olbia was the goal of this much-travelled Greek. At the time of his visit, in the middle of the fifth century, the town was experiencing a massive expansion and was the pivot of trade and traffic with the peoples of the steppe. It was the departure point of the great caravan

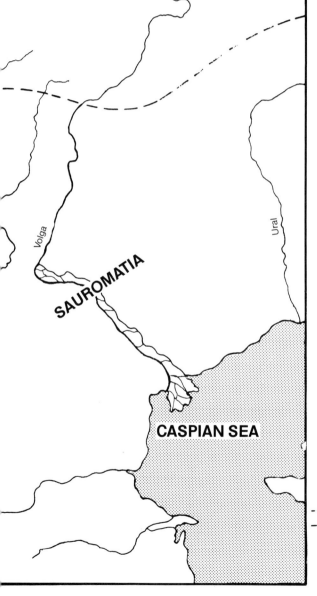

1   *Map of ancient Scythia*
------- *Boundary between forest and forest steppe*
- - - - *Boundary between forest steppe and grass steppe*
  ■ *Main Greek urban settlements on the north coast of the Black Sea*
  ● *Main fortified settlements dating from Scythian times*
  ○ *Concentrations of burial mounds*

route to the east which led far into the Asian interior and whose end was shrouded in mythical darkness, the land of the 'gold-guarding griffons' and other fabulous creatures. With the help of interpreters and middle-men, Greeks and Scythians were able to do extensive business owing to this trade route. Herodotus actually spoke to Thymnes, the Scythian King's agent in Olbia, in order to extract various items of information. On his own evidence he also visited Exampaeus, an area further inland which is still rather mysterious and which the Greeks called 'Sacred Ways'. The extent of his personal acquaintance with the actual heartland of Scythia is disputed by scholars.

Herodotus's account is one of a particularly important group of eyewitness reports. In several passages in his book he writes in the first person, so confirming his visit, which is presumed to have taken place around the middle of the fifth century BC. Another traveller who possibly visited the area a short time later wrote an account (although not a very personal one – see p. 54) which is included in the Hippocratic treatise.

A further 'eyewitness' was the unfortunate Roman poet Ovid, who after a full life in Rome close to the imperial house was exiled by Augustus to Tomis, modern Constanta in Rumania. In the year AD 9 he thus found himself directly on the western border of Scythia ('Scythia Minor'), in a town inhabited by a mixed population of 'barbarized' Greeks, Scythians and Getae. Once a flourishing Greek town, Tomis was already under immediate threat from belligerent neighbours. Wrenched from the social life of Rome, where he had belonged to the wealthy class, separated from family and friends, with no library and isolated, at first, by his inability to speak the language, Ovid led a mournful existence. In that harsh climate and in an atmosphere of war, his life was plagued by depression and illness.[3] A substantial collection of poems of lamentation (*Tristia*) and letters (*Epistulae ex Ponto*) from this last period of his life – he is said to have been buried near Tomis – has survived. They provide a wealth of information about the conditions of life in this region

at the beginning of the Christian era. The Scythians and the Sarmatians presented a constant threat to the Roman coastal province, thus causing the ageing poet additional tribulation; he described them, in the most elegant language, as particularly ugly, barbaric and lacking in culture ('not worthy of my song . . .').

Finally, in the summer of AD 95 the orator Dion Chrysostomos from Prusa in Bithynia in north-west Asia Minor journeyed to Olbia, finding there only a few remaining houses and dilapidated walls. The statues in the temple ruins and on the graves had been smashed or mutilated during barbarian attacks. The inhabitants no longer spoke pure Greek, leaving the visitor with the impression that he had strayed among backwoodsmen. The beautiful 18-year-old youth Kallistratos, who at his first meeting with Dion had just returned from a tour of duty in the steppe, wore the trousered costume of the native mounted warriors. Dion preserved his impressions of Olbia in his *Borysthenitica* ('Borysthenitian speech, delivered in my native town'), which was probably read out in Prusa. Through Dion we learn many details of life in the once flourishing town which at this late period was only a shadow of its former self. We also learn of the special relationship of the citizens of Olbia with Achilles, whom they honoured in two temples (one of which was situated on the so-called Isle of Achilles). He tells us of the poets of Olbia, who in their contests sang only of Homer. In their reverence for the great master they are said to have all been blind, since they believed one could only thus be a poet. Dion underlines his scepticism of what he heard with a joke about the contagious nature of Homer's ocular disease.

Apart from Herodotus's account in Book IV, the *Borysthenitica* is the only verifiable eyewitness report we have of a visitor to Olbia – and what changes took place in the five centuries that separate the two!

Herodotus's comments on the climate are extremely informative – indeed he gives us horrific accounts, of a sort that continue to appear in all the classical literature about the region. The Scythian cold, he says, was proverbial: the unbearably cold winter continued unabated for eight months, and the other four months were also cold and wet (according to Herodotus the cold was so severe that no horns grew on the cattle!). At the same time he describes the countryside as rich pastureland, well watered by large and beautiful rivers teeming with fish. The excellent quality of the cattle was attributed in ancient times to the famous Pontic wormwood.[4] Herodotus found the majestic *Borysthenes* (Dnieper) particularly impressive and admired the lush meadows that bordered its banks and the excellence of its water for drinking. Within the world known to him he placed it second only to the Nile in fruitfulness.

The Dnieper is still beautiful today, especially to eyes jaded by civilization. Its water is comparatively clear, often appearing a luminous blue from a distance. There is still a good stock of fish in its waters, and its banks are flanked for miles by impressive duneland and stretches of drifting sand which give the river a unique character. Like all eastern European rivers its banks are steep on the west side and flat on the east. The steep banks often reach a considerable height, and where there is a break the characteristic geological layering can be seen: a thin layer of black earth – seldom as deep as two metres – and underneath that pure loess soil, deep loam and clay.

Within the former borders of Scythia the river has, however, been completely transformed by the construction of several reservoirs ('dammed seas' in Russian). Its once famous rapids, the *Porógi*, which used to make all navigation impossible for a stretch of about 47 miles (75 km) below Dniepropetrovsk which meant unloading and continuing transport by tow-barge, have now disappeared beneath 131 ft (40 m) of dam water. It was here that the Dnieper broke through a barrier of granite gneiss caused by post-tertiary crustal movement, the 'Ukrainian horst', an eastern outcrop of the Carpathians. The impressive and dangerous nature of these rapids, which gave the Zaporogan Cossacks their name ('Cossacks of the waterfalls') and constituted a natural phenomenon unique in Europe, inspired the

Byzantine Emperor Constantine Porphyrogenetos to write a description of them in the ninth chapter of his work, *De administrando imperio*, in the tenth century.

Apart from several minor barriers, altogether seven large ones presented obstacles to navigation. The largest and most dangerous was the fourth, counting from the north; it consisted of a granite outcrop 2789 ft (850 m) in length and had a drop of 14 ft (4.3 m) down to the river bed.

Below the rapids the Dnieper formerly divided into myriad tributaries which flowed round thousands of small islands with an abundance of trees, reeds and meadows. These woods, which are often marshy, are called *plavni* and were once a paradise for birds and animals including wild boar, deer and elk. All this now belongs in the past. In the time of the Cossacks the 'capital' was situated on one of these islands, the Sitch of the Zaporogans which entered world literature with Gogol's magnificent descriptions, especially in his *Taras Bulba*. It was probably also on one of these islands that the famous defamatory letter to Sultan Mohamed IV was written, in a ribald language so well captured by Repin in his painting.[5] The letter ends: 'For which you can kiss our arses. Camp-ataman Ivan Syrko and all the camp of the Zaporogan Cossacks.'

In the north Pontic region the typical river mouth is in the form of a *liman* (lagoon), and the Dnieper is no exception. Limans are shallow, brackish estuary or coastal lakes into which the river flows from the north and which are separated from the Black Sea by a land spit. At high water the river flows over this towards the sea, but during dry periods intense evaporation causes an often evil-smelling mud basin to appear; its surface can sink several metres below sea level, and thick salt crusts form around its edges. The limans are still known for their wealth of fish, although they produced a far greater yield in ancient times. They were also a rich source of sea-salt. The Dnieper and the Bug merge in a common liman, flowing into the sea after about 19 miles (30 km).

# Nothing but grass

The land of the Scythians, that immense grass steppe moulded by wind and weather, is described by most foreigners as being dreary and depressingly monotonous with its uniformity of appearance. As mentioned above, the north Pontic steppes constitute the western outcrop of the great steppe belt which links Europe and Asia. It was the home of the European and Asiatic Scythians (Sakas) who shared it with various other tribes, which were so similar to the Scythians, however, that they can all be included in the 'Scythian world'. It is not surprising that the expression, 'the two Scythias' is therefore found in classical literature, to describe that vast tract of steppe. It stretches over a distance of about 4350 miles (7000 km) from the foot of the Carpathians all the way to Mongolia. J.G. Kohl, in the last century, used an impressive image to express the size and extent of the steppe: a calf which began its grazing in the Carpathians would only arrive at the other end of its pastureland, the foot of the Great Wall of China, when it was an ox well into maturity.

This vast expanse was nevertheless traversable, and was crossed in a relatively short time by swift troops of horsemen. Riding day and night and constantly changing horses the 'arrow riders', the elite of the Mongol dispatch-riders, covered the distance from Karakorum, the capital on the upper Orkhon, to the Hungarian plain in about one month!

If we attempt today to reconstruct these steppes and their vegetation in Scythian times, we arrive at an incomplete and indeed contradictory picture. The natural environment of ancient times has been destroyed by intense agricultural exploitation: the grassland has been replaced by enormous cultivated areas, a 'world' of sunflowers, maize and wheat. Modern canal networks traverse the countryside and are being constantly extended. Apart from the nature reserve of about 200 hectares surrounding the Askaniya-Nova zoo to the south of Kachovka, the old vegetation of the 'original' steppe has survived in only very few areas, since the flora characteristic of the steppes only establishes itself in soil left fallow for decades. If we compare various travellers' accounts – most of them from the last century – considerable differences in observation become obvious in individual descriptions. The picture is somewhat distorted by the fact that at the time the accounts were written large-scale deforestation of the steppe had already taken place. The destruction of large tracts of woodland in eastern Europe can be traced over the centuries, and we can be certain that formerly the forest area in the south was considerably greater. There was in fact a severe shortage of timber in Scythian times – doubtless exacerbated by intense overgrazing and over-exploitation of existing woodland – but Herodotus does describe amongst others a large expanse of forestland called Hylaia on the lower reaches of the Dnieper, which possibly extended eastwards as far as Molocnaya. Today there is no longer any trace of this, but travellers in the late Middle Ages still mention vestiges of it, as for instance the famous Wilhelm von Rubruk who was sent to the Mongols by the Pope in the thirteenth century and chose to take the route across the Crimea. After crossing the Taurian mountains northwards he came to a 'magnificent forest on the plain, full of springs and small streams'.[6]

In attempting to reconstruct the physical character of ancient Scythia we must also take into account the fact that not only the steppe but a considerable proportion at least of the forest steppe to the immediate north was under Scythian domination and therefore part of the Scythian landscape.

It will be seen in the following pages that there were compelling economic reasons for this bringing of steppe and forest steppe under one dominion, which was presumably achieved by means of 'fire and the sword'. The picturesque forest steppe with its undulating terrain plentifully watered by tributaries of the Dnieper such as the Sula, Psël, Vorskla, Tyasmin and Ros', its lush meadows, bushes and beautiful woodland, has always delighted travellers. By contrast, the steppe frequently induced negative reactions which in turn tended to inspire derogatory judgements with regard to the history and culture of its inhabitants.

> From time immemorial down to the present day, they [the north Pontic steppes] have been the dwelling-place of savage nomads and barbaric hordes in whom no independent seed bearing the idea of the state, the building of towns or cultural development ever took root, but who attracted the attention of the rest of the world only through their activities which were hostile to and destructive of all culture. (Kohl, 1841).

Or:

> The steppe lacks the beauty and charm of manifold vegetation.... In such desolate surroundings, where the wandering imagination finds no point of rest on the shifting horizons and the memory no place whereby it can orientate itself, there is also a lack of historical legend ... in comparison with western Europe, eastern Europe has little to offer. There is only too frequently a barbaric quality about the latter, in ancient times as in the Middle Ages. In our continent the light rises in the west and disappears in the east. (Roesler, 1863)

The colonization of the southern Ukraine from Russia was therefore welcomed as the 'curing of the steppe sickness'. The fertile land was transformed into a granary. In spite of the retention of livestock-breeding, land cultivation became so widespread that the former features of the landscape were changed out of all recognition.

A rich source of information for the archaeologist wishing to reconstruct the ancient topography is provided by the geological deposits of the large burial mounds. Since their slopes are frequently too steep for cultivation, the old vegetation has survived on their surface and often around their base. It both illustrates and verifies the descriptions of earlier centuries, enabling us to imagine in detail the 'bottomless sea' into which the writers gazed:

> For a few versts one sees nothing but wormwood and more wormwood, then nothing but vetch for a few versts, then half a mile of mullein and another half of melilot, then an expanse of swaying milkweed, a thousand million nodding heads, then sage and lavender for the duration of an afternoon doze, then tulips as far as the eye can see, a bed of mignonette two miles across, whole valleys of caraway and curled mint, endless hills covered in resurrection plant and six days' journey with nothing but dried-up grass. This is the way vegetation is more or less distributed in the steppe, with a complete lack of charm, beauty or attractive feature of any kind.

Thus the German traveller J.G. Kohl describes his impressions of the steppe region of the Ukraine in 1841 (and sighed inwardly: 'If only there were alpine meadows, or even the grass of the Black Forest or the Odenwald, or the lawns of the green island of Britain!'). On the subject of spring in the steppe (towards the middle of April) he remarks:

> ... and to embark on a spring campaign in the steppe with Mongols or Tatars has of course its attractions. But only with nomads; for living amongst tillers of the soil in the steppe is unbearable even in the springtime. It is a mystery how a man could think of settling as a farmer in the steppe whose whole nature cries out against this abuse, whose whole law is movement, whose soil abhors deep-rooted plants, favouring instead mobile cattle-breeding, whose winds carry everything before them far and wide and whose flatness invites everything to cross it in haste.

We come here to an essential point: it is clear that an understanding of the steppe was only possible from the perspective of the horse-rider. It seems that it was only on the hardy and swift steppe horses, which used to be kept half wild in nomadic studs, that it was possible to experience the feeling of life in the steppe, the hardships and also the special delights of the nomadic horseman's existence. This is reflected in Russian literature, as well as in the literature of western Europe.

The steppe is indeed oppressive for anyone on foot, forcing him to move at a snail's pace, especially when the terrain is rendered impassable by downpours of rain; at best, the distances shrink when measured by the speed of a hardy horse moving at a gallop. This still holds good today. The modern archaeologist, descending from the expedition lorry after a long, bone-shaking stretch of uneven steppe track, covered in the ubiquitous black-earth dust, differs only slightly from the nineteenth-century traveller who tried to cross the steppe in a cart drawn by horses or oxen and similarly suffered from aching muscles.

Nowadays the inclemency of the weather is of course easier to cope with, but winter is protracted in the steppe and often punctuated by severe snow storms (the *v'jugas*) which usually last for three days and nights. Such storms were always particularly dangerous in the steppe, which offered no protection, and could drive the herds into one of the numerous loess ravines or even to the edge of the steppe plateau from which animals and men not infrequently hurtled into the sea. Because of the storms Black Sea maritime traffic used to be halted in winter, usually for several months. The harbours and even the open sea froze over for several kilometres out from the shore, so that you could travel for instance from Odessa to the Crimea over the ice. (Herodotus gives us similar information about Scythian times.) The protraction of the winter is particularly wearing: the snow storms start towards the end of October, and November is already almost a winter month proper. 'Real' winter lasts from December to February or March. Spring does not begin until about the middle of April (as opposed to the Caspian steppes in the east, where it starts as early as February), but when it does it is luxuriant. The end of April and beginning of May is the most pleasant season, with rain in abundance, and in June it becomes drier. In July there is practically no moisture; there are hardly any storms, usually only storm-like electrical discharges with thunder and lightning but no rain. From the end of July until well into August the drought period reaches its peak.

Today artificial irrigation alleviates the worst of the drought, but in the past it was a time of suffering for everything living. The steppe was turned into a desert waste, dark brown to black in colour, where deceptive mirages gave the illusion of lakes and expanses of water. Wells and springs dried up. If winter was a time of hunger for the cattle (since methods of food storage had not been developed), summer was a time of thirst.

The rains which fall in the second half of August have the effect almost of a second spring in the steppe. It becomes green again, and everything recovers under a strikingly beautiful sky ('O how feeble is all our cloud theory in comparison with the wealth of form to be seen in a single autumn evening sky in the steppes!' Kohl, 1841). At the end of September the weather becomes dull; rain and mist set in. In the open steppe there is hardly an autumn in our sense of the word: winter comes almost without transition. It may have been somewhat different in ancient times, however, since the forest area was larger. One can well imagine that the constitution and mentality of the ancient inhabitants was moulded by the climate and landscape of the steppe. Certainly the Scythian steppe would not have appealed to a particularly refined taste, but with its wildness, unrestricted open spaces and untamed flora it must nevertheless have exerted a strong attraction. Flocks of eagles, vultures, falcons and hawks flew across the sky. The horses sank up to their knees in a swaying silvery sea of side oats and of silkweed in particular, and myriads of mullein flowers, the 'lights of the steppe', accompanied the rider on his way, their arms spread like candelabra. There were tall forests of hemp and spurge. As late as the last century, bunches of irises and tulips, hyacinths and crocuses adorned every dwelling, every holy picture, youths and girls, and even the horses.

More than anything else the Scythian air was permeated by the slightly bitter aroma of wormwood. It grew higher than a man, and can still be found today. The larks of the steppe can also still be heard warbling in the skies. And when you meet herds of cattle, tended by kolkhozniks, when the dust swirls up and the lowing of hundreds of cattle is heard, you can almost feel you are back in ancient Scythia.

# 2 Death and burial

## The pyramids of the steppe

The Scythians are by no means the only nomadic horse-riding people to have inhabited the vast north Pontic steppes, but they represent the earliest known incursion from the east. They were followed, amongst others, by Sarmatians, Huns, Pechenegae, Hungarians, Polovci and Mongols. For most of these peoples this part of the steppe was only a transit stage on their long journey to the west, and there are only very few archaeological remains relating to them. It is a different matter with those peoples who chose the region north of the Black Sea as their permanent home. Countless burial mounds, called *kurgany* in eastern Europe and *mogily* in the Ukraine, bear witness to their presence. The Scythian kurgans are the highest and can usually be distinguished from the others by their outward form as indeed by their whole structure. They reach the imposing height of three-storey buildings, whereby the base can extend to a diameter of over 328 ft (100 m). They are usually arranged in groups, often consisting of a particularly high mound surrounded by smaller ones. In certain areas they are so concentrated that we may

2 *Group of mounds surrounding the Perepyaticha kurgan, with Bronze Age and early Iron Age burials (Kohn and Mehlis).*

3    *The 69 ft (21 m) high Aleksandropol' kurgan before its excavation in 1852–6* (Drevnosti Gerodotovoi Skifii).

speak of a 'grave landscape' – as far as the eye can see: hundreds, sometimes thousands of mounds, whose contours, in spite of intensive cultivation, are still clearly recognizable. Today they have to a large extent been ploughed over, however, and would at best only be visible from the air.

In the steppe plain the kurgans stand out particularly clearly from their environment and can often be seen for miles. In earlier times they acted as important landmarks and defence positions. They are surrounded by many romantic and sometimes gruesome legends telling of golden treasures and other precious objects contained within them which can be won by the bold-hearted. According to folk tradition, light and noise have been known to filter out from the carousing and celebrations of the dead. Some of the mounds bear romantic names such as the famous Solocha kurgan (water-nymph hill), where in 1914 archaeologists found an undisturbed royal grave. Some have much more prosaic names such as Tolstaya mogila (broad burial mound), Kozël (goat) or Orël (eagle) kurgan.

These remarkable mounds have aroused interest since very early on, and archaeological excavations began in the eighteenth century. The sole intention, however, was usually to remove the precious objects from the tombs. There are consequently very few records, so that the scientific value of some of the magnificent gold finds was limited. If the Russian tsars, starting with Peter the Great, had not taken an interest in these unique products of Scythian times, strangely barbaric and yet so striking and fascinating in their effect, it is probable that most of the now famous objects of animal art would long ago have been melted down for their considerable weight in gold. What could be saved found its way indirectly into the Hermitage and today constitutes one of the most impressive treasure stores in the world.

The conspicuous burial mounds with their wealth of treasure inside also attracted bands of grave-robbers, however. They penetrated into the tombs in spite of the risks and often with great difficulty, to the despair of the modern archaeologist who is constantly find-

20

ing traces of them. The sacrilege and plundering of graves is not a modern invention: we know of its occurrence in ancient times, and sometimes it is possible to determine almost precisely when it took place. Their activities in the dark cost some of the robbers their lives, and their skeletons were found during later scientific excavations and could thus be examined. The evidence shows what happened: the pressure of the earth above them took the robbers by surprise, crushing or suffocating them. In one case they even remained upright, picks and spades in their hands; the remnants of a purse containing small coins of the period of Mithradates VI Eupator (107–63 BC) at their feet make an approximate dating possible. Fortunately for archaeology, blind fear and superstition seem in some cases to have deterred the accomplices of those killed from further incursion into the tombs. This is the only explanation for the fact that the most important tomb of Scythian times, the imposing Čertomlyk kurgan, was found for the most part intact by its excavator Zabelin in the middle of the last century. A dead grave-robber, found in one of the chambers, could have been the reason for this.

We shall now examine the tomb layout more closely. From the fifth century BC the typical form of tomb in the Scythian steppes was the 'catacomb'. The term is in accordance with Russian tradition and has no relation to our idea of catacombs which derives mainly from the subterranean burial grounds of the early Christians in Rome. The south Russian catacomb graves are, however, similarly characterized by their subterranean position and the earth covering of the burial chamber.

The basic structural principle of the catacomb graves, which can, however, differ widely in the way in which they are hollowed out, consists of a descent, usually leading steeply down from the original surface, with a corridor or short passage below opening into a cave-like burial chamber. The descent usually has steps going down the side, which made access easier; this was certainly necessary, since not only the dead body itself but

4   *Plan of a catacomb grave*

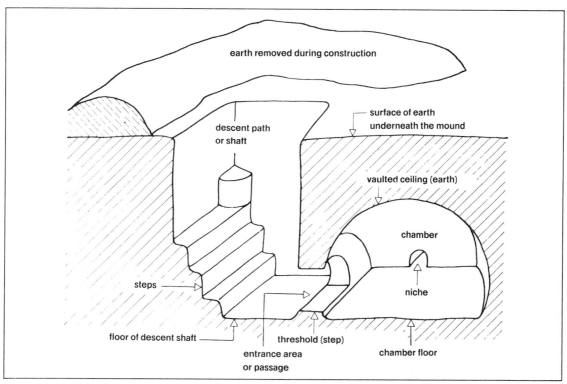

also all of its equipment for the next world had to be laboriously transported down.

The reckless daring of the grave-robbers becomes particularly clear when one considers the extremely complicated structure of the tombs of the Scythian ruling class. The descents are in fact shafts which go down between 33 and 49 feet deep (10–15 m). The underground passages are sometimes like tunnels, reaching the considerable length of 98 ft (30 m) and occasionally branching off. Sometimes they are short, however, forming vaulted entrances. The chambers themselves are spacious, usually rounded, hollowed-out areas, and further side-chambers, alcoves and other recesses are built into the walls.

In their basic architectual conception these often extensive cavern systems of the catacomb

5  *Timber-lined entrance shaft in the Drana Kochta kurgan (Zeltokamenka) during the excavation in 1974.*

graves were only possible owing to the firmness of the loess and loam earth from which they were constructed. Tons of soil had to be dug out and transported, sometimes as much as 14,126 cubic ft (400 cubic m) if it was for the tomb of a king or prince.

After the burial the descent path or shaft of the tomb was filled in. The chamber itself where the body lay remained open, and when the burial rites were over it was merely blocked with the dismantled parts of the funeral car on which the dead body and its equipment had been transported. Above the shaft, which was filled in with earth or large rocks, the burial mound was gradually raised.

This method of burial meant that such a catacomb grave was only technically possible for the interment of those who had died or been killed at the same time as each other. Once the grave shaft had been filled in, it could only have been opened up again with the aid of complicated support apparatus and at the expense of an inordinate amount of time such as is necessary for modern excavations. If for some reason the Scythians wished to bury another body in a tomb which had been filled in, they dug a second shaft and tunnelled through from the bottom until – with luck – they came to the original burial chamber. Here, without disturbing the first burial, they laid the body of the person who had died later.

This process required of course a precise knowledge of the position of the first burial and also a good sense of direction under ground. Since at first sight some of these second approaches were structurally similar to those tunnelled by the grave-robbers, their significance was for a long time lost on archaeologists. This was compounded in some mounds where apart from the central graves there are also side graves, adding to the confusion. It is only in recent years that excavations making use of soil samples and detailed analysis of traces of ancient workings have been able to establish the facts more precisely.

Taking the example of the Tolstaya mogila mound of Ordžonikidze, excavated in 1971, we shall now follow the working procedure of

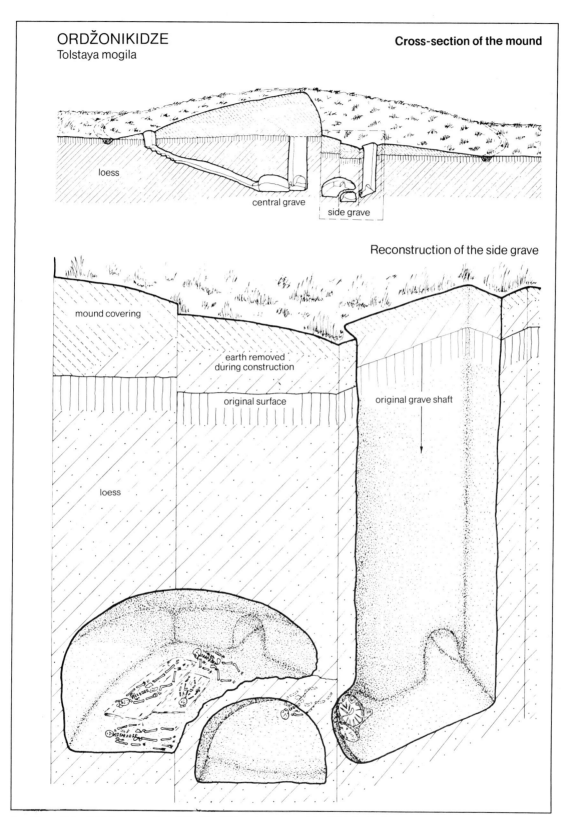

### ORDŽONIKIDZE
Tolstaya mogila

**Cross-section of the mound**

loess

central grave

side grave

**Reconstruction of the side grave**

mound covering

earth removed
during construction

original surface

original grave shaft

loess

6   *Plan of the Tolstaya mogila of Ordžonikidze, investigated in 1971 by B.N. Mozolevski.*

a modern excavation in the steppe region:

1. After careful examination of the mound earth, carried out with the help of bulldozers, all half a million cubic ft (15,000 cubic m) of it is removed apart from a (trimmed) central section which is left standing for purposes of analysis. The cross-section of this reveals a pointed, almost triangular accumulation of yellow to reddish-brown earth. This is the soil which was removed from the grave and not used to fill in the shaft but heaped around the shaft opening and stamped firm – apparently a strictly observed ritual, the meaning of which has not yet been deciphered.

This ring of earth has openings for 'processional paths', by which the grave could be approached. During the excavations these paths often stand out clearly on the original surface, and sometimes they can be traced for long stretches. To avoid the risk of the ceremonial funeral car sticking in the mud, reeds and stakes or similar material were placed along the processional paths.

On the original surface a rectangular, almost black discoloration can be seen in the yellow loess – a signal for the archaeologists that it is here that they have to dig down, as this discoloration marks the upper opening of the grave shaft which was filled in after the burial. The Tolstaya mogila contained two graves similar in principle, one central grave and a side grave which was added later, and was thus a kind of 'family tomb' (see p. 23).

2. The excavation continues 'by hand'. In order to expose the grave layout, the so-called 'negative excavation technique' is used as far as possible. This is probably one of the most timesaving methods available for this difficult type of grave, and does not destroy the original structure. The dark discolorations are followed when digging down, and the earth used for filling in is carefully lifted out, so that the contours of the original grave remain, in negative form. Whereas the untouched earth which forms the shaft walls is relatively firm, the earth used to fill in the shaft can be removed without difficulty.

3. If the excavators have been careful enough, traces of the ancient workings from Scythian times can be observed on the walls of the shaft. The grave-diggers of that time worked with square-shaped axes or with long tools similar to our modern pointed pick-axes (also one of the most deadly weapons in hand-to-hand fighting) and the imprints of these can be clearly seen.

4. Near the bottom of the shaft in one of the walls one can see the arched opening to the passage which leads to the burial chamber.

5. The exposing of catacomb graves poses extreme technical problems. The shaft and also all underground passages and chambers have to be expertly supported during the excavation, for which the help of miners and mining engineers is necessary. They also have to be secured against water penetration caused by the sudden downpours which are so violent in central Europe. The excavation process is particularly difficult if parts of the old burial chamber and its outer rooms are buried in tons of earth. This may have happened over the millennia but can be exacerbated by the vibrations of the bulldozers during the removal of the mound. This mass of earth has to be removed with cranes.

6. Excavation work in the passage. On page 25 the wheels of the dismantled funeral car are being cleaned. The wooden parts and rusty iron ferrules were in such fragile condition that they could only be exposed by carefully blowing away the earth which covered them. Beside the waggon wheels lies the skeleton of the 'waggon-driver' who had been killed for the burial. The chamber can be seen in the background.

7. Fig. 6 shows a view of the side-grave chamber in the Ordžonikidze kurgan. It contained five burials: that of a young woman (No. 1), very richly equipped, and of an infant of about two years with similarly precious burial gifts (No. 2); at their head lies a skeleton of a strapping young man (No. 3), who was probably meant to be their 'weapon-bearer' or 'protector' in the next world since he was the only one equipped with bow and arrow. He had been killed during the funeral ceremonies by having his skull crushed. At the feet of the two main burial figures lies the skeleton of a young and probably female person (No. 4), assumed by the excavators to

7 Excavation work in the passage of the side grave of the Tolstaya mogila. In the foreground are waggon wheels and the skeleton of the 'waggon driver' who had been sacrificed.

8 Uncovering a magnificent sword in the central grave of the mound. See front cover for detail of the scabbard, which is decorated with scenes of fighting animals.

9  View of the completely exposed burial chamber of the side grave in the Tolstaya mogila, artificially supported by wooden posts. For an explanation of the numbers, see pp. 24 and 27.

10  Household niche of the grave, with kitchen equipment and remains of food. In the foreground is skeleton No. 4.

have been a 'nurse' or 'kitchen maid' since she lies immediately outside the entrance to the kitchen niche containing food offerings and cooking utensils. The fifth skeleton, that of the 'waggon-driver', lies in the foreground and is therefore not visible here.

Originally the graves were always above ground water level, and can only have become waterlogged after a later rise in that level. We should not in fact base our assumptions on present-day soil conditions and imagine that these underground chambers were dark, damp caves. The subterranean soil in which the catacomb graves were constructed consists of pale, often pastel-coloured to almost white loess. Archaeological investigations have shown that with the help of lighting, sources of heat such as small portable stoves, colourful wall-hangings and carpets, furs and other frequently costly furnishings, a reasonably comfortable interior was created in these 'dwellings of the dead'. Everything was provided that could contribute to comfort in the next world – cushions and pillows stuffed with eelgrass and moss to support head and legs, and mattresses like beds, to rest on.

## The King is dead! The waggon journey to Gerrhus and the events on the fortieth day

After this survey of the grave interiors we shall look at the funeral ceremonies – taking a royal burial as an example – as far as they can be reconstructed from archaeological finds and written sources.

According to Herodotus's graphic description (IV, 71), the Scythians followed an interesting procedure when embalming their kings. The body was cut open, the innards removed and the cavity cleaned. This was then filled with aromatic spices and sewn up again. Finally the body was coated with wax.

The main purpose of such preservation methods was probably to maintain the body of the dead king in a reasonable condition for the ceremonial waggon journey to the various regions of his dominions, and to demonstrate and make possible his uncorrupted bodily presence at the numerous feasts held in his honour. There were 40 days between death and burial, we learn from written sources, and it seems certain that this period, so important in all Indo-European funeral customs, was also strictly observed in Scythian burial rites. According to traditional folk belief, after 40 days the soul leaves the body, where it has been hovering, and departs for the land of the dead. For some peoples in ancient times and also in the Middle Ages, this occurred on the thirtieth or fortieth day after death (for the peoples of eastern Europe it was predominantly the fortieth day). This belief was so fundamental that it persisted until modern times in eastern European Christianity. Written sources relating to peoples of ancient times have shown that the dead person was considered to be a 'living corpse' during that time; among other things he still had administrative charge over his possessions and was held to be sexually potent, so that his marriage was still valid over this period. Only after the fortieth day did this living corpse change into one of the 'living dead'. According to this belief there was therefore no death in the absolute sense.

Against this background much can be understood about Scythian burial customs: the fitting out of the graves as 'dwellings', the placing there of sometimes very considerable possessions (doubtless also from a fear that the 'living dead body' might become angry if it were the victim of dishonesty, and wreak terrible revenge), the offering of lavish sacrifices in honour of the dead, and the provision of everything which might please, amuse, occupy or perhaps distract them. This was all no doubt accompanied by a deep underlying fear of the 'living dead' – those who, having suffered unjust treatment, cannot rest in their graves and so return to harm the living. On the other hand there would also have been a joyful remembrance of those dead who were thought of as content in their extremely pleasant surroundings underground, and whose help and support could always be relied upon if rich sacrificial offerings were made on later occasions.

This idea of the next world as a rosy version of this world probably precluded the thought of mourning in our sense of the word.

Unfortunately not one embalmed Scythian body has survived the ravages of the centuries. By an unusually fortuitous circumstance however, preservation through 'perpetual ice', carefully prepared human bodies from the extreme east of the Scythian world have survived. These are presumably not 'genuine' Scythians but members of closely related tribes which buried their dead in the high Altai. The finds from the kurgans of Pazyryk, which had to be painstakingly defrosted, are world-famous owing to their unique state of preservation and their wealth of organic material. (We shall return to these at a later stage.) Those buried in these graves had been lavishly prepared: the skull was trepanned and the brain removed, the bodies were cut open so that the innards could be taken out, then sewn up again. In addition, the arm and leg muscles were removed by means of a number of horizontal and vertical incisions and replaced by another substance. The location of such incisions varied according to whether the body was male or female.

Unfortunately the various substances inside the bodies have not been analysed and we cannot therefore ascertain whether they bear any resemblance to those described by Herodotus. The bodies found in Pazyryk suggest a social gradation which may have been manifested – as was the case in Egypt – in the varying degrees of lavishness and costliness of the conservation. It is probable that the European Scythians also preserved not only the bodies of kings from corruption (although with a particularly costly substance in their case) but preserved other bodies too, above all those 'living corpses' which were driven round the country for 40 days and taken to feasts. Under the climatic conditions of the steppe region in the summer months, with temperatures of between 70–85° F (20–30° C) or more, a corpse which had not been preserved would have passed through its worst phase of decomposition, and it would hardly have been possible to drive it round with the proper ceremony and endure its presence at the various farewell feasts – even presupposing the greatest possible 'toughness' of those participating. The obligatory period of 40 days made preservation measures essential, especially since for the ceremonial presentation horse carcases were also preserved – the abdominal cavity being emptied, cleaned, and filled with chaff.

It is again to Herodotus that we owe the description of such a preparation (IV, 72); following his precise account of the burial of a king, he adds various details of the death cult which ensued. This involved the setting up one year later of 'spectral riders' around the mound which had been raised. For this procedure 50 chosen servants and 50 of the finest horses were strangled and preserved by cleaning out the abdominal cavity and filling it with chaff. Stakes were then driven through both horses and men and fixed together in such a way that the bodies of the men, supported by the wooden poles, sat straight up as if mounted on the backs of the horses. Finally these dead riders and their bridled mounts were fixed to supports made of waggon wheels which had been fitted together, so that the bodies would remain in this position for a considerable time afterwards. Seen from a distance these riders, arranged in a circle round the foot of the mound, must have given the eerie impression of being alive.

Since Herodotus's terms are difficult to translate, his description of the embalming ingredients has led to vigorous scholarly debate. The plants used were probably galingale or saffron, incense plants, celery and anise. The filling of the body with these plant substances was of only secondary importance, however, the prime practical purpose being presumably to stifle the smell of the corpse. The essential measures were in fact the emptying of the abdominal cavity in order to inhibit decomposition, setting off the process of mummification through dessication, and the outer wax coating which prevented the penetration of maggots. The wax which had hardened on to the human skin doubtless made it possible for cosmetics to be used on the corpse, so that the face of the dead body might have appeared almost normal.

The Scythians probably used honey as well as wax in the preservation of corpses. The antibacterial properties of honey were well known in antiquity and it was widely used, especially in the orient. Honey was also an ingredient in the embalming of Alexander the Great, for example.

Preservation in honey is extremely effective for a limited period. Even in the late Middle Ages it was the best method of transporting almost intact the heads of the 'giaours', severed outside the gates of Vienna, on the long journey to Istanbul where they could be displayed before the Sultan in identifiable condition.

The Scythian graves reflect the social organization of the time. According to the prevailing conception of the next world, the social structure of this world was clearly translated into life after death, although there might have been the possibility of a 'social climb' in the grave. We know from the Thracians, who were immediate neighbours of the Scythians, that after the death of a warrior his wives quarrelled violently over which of them was to follow the dead man into the grave, for it was assumed that she was the one he had loved most. The one finally chosen was ceremonially led to the grave, killed by her closest kinsmen and buried with her husband. Within the context of Scythian belief it may well also have denoted prestige for a young servant girl to accompany a renowned old warrior into the next world as his wife, so that the victims would have offered themselves for sacrifice more or less voluntarily. And the belief that they would be making their entrance into the land of the living dead as part of the princely household of a magnificently equipped ruler may have considerably lessened the horror of a violent death, and it is possible that they were helped along with some kind of anaesthetic.

Excavators examining the skeletons of those killed in order to accompany the dead person, have made numerous observations which throw an interesting light on their last moments of life: crushed skulls, blows on the temple, and in two cases the hands were dug into the ground. The floor surface of carpeting and wood ensured that this attitude was preserved and that the hands did not open even after the rigor mortis period. Several skeletons were found arm in arm or hand in hand. Various factors indicate that even sexual acts cannot be ruled out as part of the funeral rites.

The side grave of the Tolstaya mogila of Ordžonikidze, mentioned above, is of such vital importance to Scythian research because it was never plundered by grave-robbers. It was therefore possible for the first time to make precise observations in a complex multiphase grave in line with modern scientific requirements. Amongst other things it contains the remains of a child, two years of age at most, who had been buried later in extreme luxury. This child had costly funeral gifts similar to those of an adult, but in miniature; even the jewellery and details of the clothing were on a much smaller scale and corresponded to his age. One object, however, was definitely an exception: in his right hand the child clutched a heavy gold adult-size armring which his tiny fingers had held demonstratively upright until he was found by the excavators, still in this attitude.

This very striking hand position, as if proffering the article of jewellery, was clearly intended by those in charge of the burial operations, and therefore of some significance. Its meaning may be derived from the following hypothesis. The Tolstaya mogila contained, as a kind of tomb, the remains of a Scythian royal family together with servants and horses. Two separate graves had been constructed one after the other; first a central grave, after the death of the prince, over which the mound was raised. Shortly afterwards – the grass had hardly begun to grow on the mound, as its section shows – came the death of the much younger woman, who was laid in the side grave bored especially for her. She was doubtless a close relative of the prince in the central grave (who was at least fifty years of age) – most probably his wife or at any rate one of his wives. Not long after that the child died, a second entrance to the side grave was dug with enormous expenditure of labour, and the child was laid on the right side of the young

11 *The 5th Pazyryk kurgan during the excavation in 1949 (Rudenko). After the removal of the mound of stones, the timber construction is exposed: beneath the wooden ceiling is the ice-filled timber chamber.*

12 *The male burial in the 5th Pazyryk kurgan in the tree coffin in situ (Rudenko). The coffin originally also contained the mummy of a woman, but this had been half dragged out by grave-robbers.*

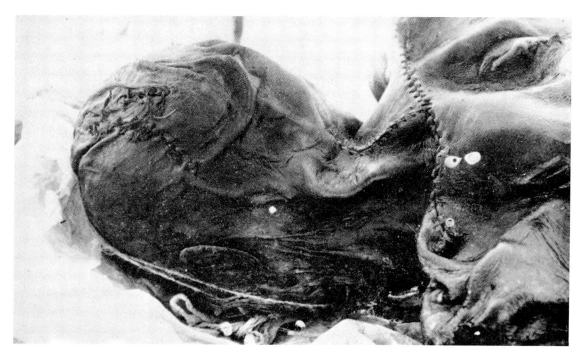

13 *Position of embalming incisions in the back of the woman from the 5th kurgan. The skull had been trepanned and the incision in the scalp carefully sewn up again, as with the operations on the other parts of the body.*

14 *By comparison, the stitches in the back of the man from the same kurgan. It is not clear why the muscles were removed. Rudenko suggests that this may have been a practice connected with endocannibalism.*

woman who was therefore in all probability its mother. The woman's skeleton was literally laden with gold jewellery: she had eleven rings on her fingers and three gold armrings on her arms – two on the right wrist and one on the left. They were of the same type as that held by the child, though very much lighter. Had the child perhaps inherited the armring from its mother, who for this reason had been buried wearing only three armrings? Did the young woman die giving birth to the child, which afterwards followed her to the grave? At all events a certain period of time had elapsed during which the dead woman had not seen her child. Did the latter therefore have to 'identify himself' in order for her to accept him in the grave as her own child? In the eyes of the living, was it perhaps the woman herself who had summoned the child to her, a notion similar to other ancient folk beliefs?

## Pasture for all eternity

The raising of mounds was an organized communal activity. The height of the burial mound probably depended on the social station or rank of the deceased. As a general rule, the higher the kurgan, the more extensive the grave material and the more lavish the traces of ceremonial sacrifice at its base. In some cases, however, rich graves have been discovered underneath quite insignificant mounds. Either the raising of the mound did not take place here for some important reason, possibly a military campaign or the like, or it could be that the dead person was not entitled to a high mound for some reason of which we have no knowledge.

Scythian burial mounds of the Ukrainian steppes are characterized by one very striking factor: they almost always consist of pure black earth. If one of the high mounds is observed from a distance, it is noticeable that the ground around it has not been disturbed, as would be apparent after the removal of such a large quantity of earth. Bronze Age mounds are by comparison usually surrounded by a more or less large, trough-like

depression; it follows that their mounds were constructed quite differently.

Since the black-earth topsoil represents only a relatively shallow upper layer (usually 2.6 ft (0.80 m) to 4 ft (1.20 m) thick, while the high mounds contain half a million cubic ft (15,000 cubic m) of soil, the question arises of where this enormous quantity of earth came from if not from the immediate vicinity. By a fortunate chance, during the recent excavations in Ordžonikidze light was shed for the first time on this obscure mystery. Soil samples showed here that the black earth of the high mound contained a proportion of manganese only met with $2\frac{1}{2}$ miles (4 km) away. It is therefore clear that the material for the mounds was transported from relatively distant locations.

It was characteristic of the Scythians to expend vast amounts of labour and energy on the work necessary to construct their graves. During the excavations in the Sakan necropolis of Bessatyr, in the seven-river region of Kazakhstan, it was ascertained for the first time that the tree trunks used to build the large burial chambers (see fig. 15) must have been transported from a location approximately 125 miles (200 km) away. The most recent examination of the huge Aržan kurgan in Tuva (see figs. 18 and 19) has shown that 6000 trunks of selected 100 year-old larches were brought to the site for the building of the tomb. But the question remains, why did they find it necessary to transport *earth* from such distances? The latest analyses provide a somewhat surprising answer. The structure of the burial mounds, which at first sight appeared to be simple – if colossal – heaps of earth, proved to be architectural. The 'pyramids of the steppe' were basically constructed from pieces of turf which were carefully built up one on top of the other. At the core of the mound this layering can be closely observed.

In the light of this our ideas on the construction of the burial mounds have to be thoroughly revised, since it was obviously not as arbitrary a procedure as had been assumed, but followed a significant plan. If we take as an example the Tolstaya mogila burial mound of Ordžonikidze, whose underground layout

15    *Timber burial chamber in kurgan 6 of Bešatyr, Kazakhstan (Akišev).*

we observed during its excavation, it consisted of about half a million cubic ft (15,000 cubic m) of black earth and is therefore classed as a medium-sized Scythian royal burial mound. The realization that this mass of earth consists of pieces of turf (about 6 in. (15 cm) thick) leads us to calculate that half a million cubic ft (15,000 cubic m) means a million sq ft (99,000 sq m) or, as a piece of grassland, an area of about 10.33 × 10.33 sq ft (315 x 315 m).

As we have shown above, the funeral rites of the Scythians were particularly life-orientated in their underlying ideas and procedures. The finality of death was unknown to them, and it was essential that the person who had passed over into the next world should continue his existence in the most pleasant conditions possible, that is, those which corresponded closely to his circumstances in this world. A dead Scythian whose weapons, tools as well as animals were placed in the grave with him would of course urgently require pasture in the next world. And that is just what the burial mound appears to have been: symbolic pasture, which varied in size according to the dead person's social station, possessions and esteem. The idea of the next world as a kind of 'heavenly pasture' is by no means uncommon. In this respect the Scythian prince from the Tolstaya mogila finds himself in the company of the Hittite king whose elaborate funeral, lasting many days, is recorded in cuneiform texts: 'Now O Sungod, ensure that this pasture remains his rightful property! And no-one shall wrest it from him [or] make legal claim to it! And on this pasture cattle and sheep, horses and mules shall graze for him!'[7] This was declared on the eighth day of the ceremonies, and the dead king was brought many cattle and a piece of actual turf which, with the help of magic rites, would accompany him into the next world.

Further research on the Scythian mounds will reveal in more detail the background to this primitive idea of the next world. Soil samples have shown that the pieces of turf must have been of particularly rich grassland from estuary flats, which were cut and heaped up as a monument to the deceased. This could mean that the area of pasture, far from being arbitrarily selected, had to be a particular and perhaps highly valued lush meadow, which would therefore sometimes necessitate transport from some distance – in the case of Ordžonikidze, 2½ miles (4 km) or even further.

Marco Polo informs us that the Mongol rulers of a later age were buried in places to which they were particularly attached in their lifetimes. It is possible that the choice of site for the Scythian burial mounds was determined by similar considerations.

We owe a further important discovery to the excavations of the Tolstaya mogila of Ordžonikidze. For the first time, in painstaking detail, the entire soil content of a circular ditch surrounding the foot of the mound was examined. This was possible only with the greatest difficulty, since the earth that filled the ditch – black earth washed down from the mound – proved to be a sticky, black, almost rock-hard mass which at times had to be softened inch by inch in order to recover the large amount of bones within it. The plan of the excavation (see fig. 16) shows 11 substantial concentrations of animal bones (although the west section has been obliterated by the construction of roads and a railway line). Their careful examination by the palaeozoologist B.I. Bibikova in Kiev later resulted in one of the most dramatic discoveries of this mound, which is certainly not lacking in sensational finds. The results of her investigation were the remains of 35 horses, 14 wild boar and 2 stags. According to the stratigraphic findings the animal remains may have originated either from one large funeral feast or from several, although these must have taken place at very short intervals.

As mentioned above, a good part of the animal bones was lost through the destruction of the ditch. Our findings therefore represent only a minimum proportion of the original deposit. If, however, we take just the quantity of animal bones which have survived and calculate the weight in meat of the slaughtered beasts, we arrive at the princely amount – allowing for various sources of error – of 14,330 pounds (6,500 kilos) of meat! We know from parallels in the field of ethnology – in Central Asia and Siberia for example, where such funeral feasts were traditionally held right into the twentieth century – that the amount of meat consumed by each participant was about 11 pounds (5 kilos) a day.

Basing her calculations on this, Bibikova concludes that at least 1300 people must have taken part in the feast at the Tolstaya mogila. This figure obviously makes us aware of the size of the workforce which constructed the mound, for we know that this was done voluntarily by members of the dead man's tribe.

The funeral feast must certainly have been preceded by a wild boar and stag hunt on a very large scale. Huge quantitites of amphora shards show that it was not just a matter of massive meat consumption. After the feast the wine containers were presumably smashed, although a proportion of them were placed upright with their bases embedded in the earth. Thirteen such amphora bases were found still buried where they served as drink offerings for the dead man – or perhaps rather

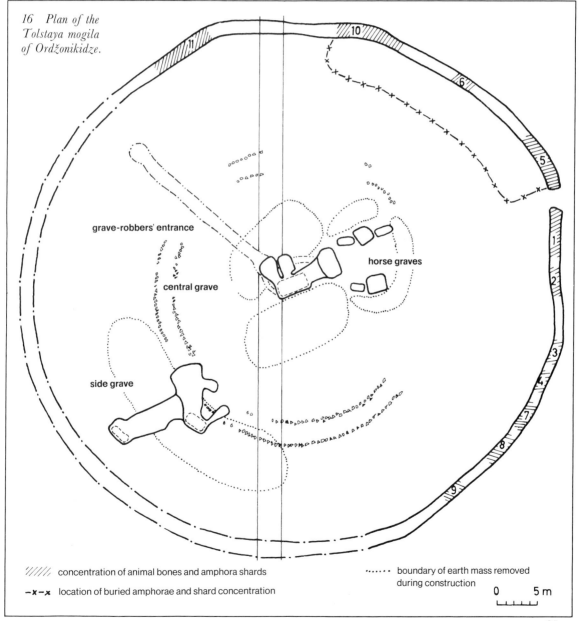

*16 Plan of the Tolstaya mogila of Ordžonikidze.*

grave-robbers' entrance

horse graves

central grave

side grave

////// concentration of animal bones and amphora shards

−x−x location of buried amphorae and shard concentration

••••••• boundary of earth mass removed during construction

0      5 m

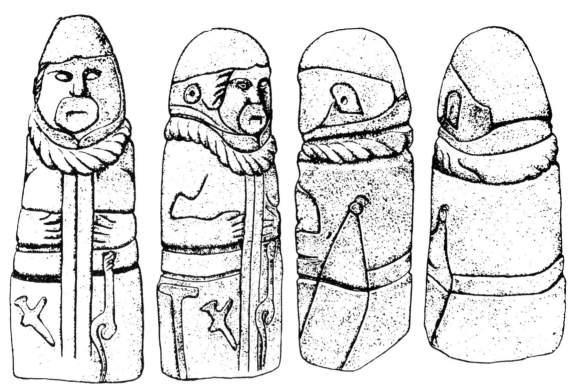

17 *Armed warriors with neck rings.* Scythian kamennaya baba *from Ol'chovčik Oblast' Doneck (Tachtay).* *Height 26.4 in. (0.67 m). A helmet, short sword and whip hanging from the belt are recognizable from the front.*

as a sign that his health had been well and truly drunk.

In many cases a large stone human figure had originally stood on top of the burial mound. Although we know of numerous such stone stelae, only one of them has actually been found upright and still intact on a Scythian kurgan. Most of them had fallen down and lay beside or in the base of the mound, or were carried away or smashed to pieces as 'heathen idolatry'. Often they were simply exchanged, being later replaced by another figure; the custom of setting up stone idols of this kind on graves, of venerating them and attributing miraculous powers to them, was widespread among the peoples of Eurasia. It began as early as the Neolithic age and continued into the late Middle Ages. Several thousand of these large primitive statues are known to us; many are crudely fashioned, with human features only roughly indicated, but often the sculpture is magnificent and impressive. The most well known are the

numerous stone idols of the Polovci, a nomadic people who dominated the north Pontic steppe from the eleventh to the thirteenth century AD. Their stone figures, often portraying the men, as well as the women, with outsize breasts and bellies, led to the Russian popular term *kamennaya baba* ('stone woman') which was applied to all such idols.

The Scythian *kamennye baby* are however exclusively male, usually warriors – often with phallus emphasized – who carry weapons and wear jewellery. The portrayal of the weapon types is so precise that the figures can be clearly defined and dated accordingly. However, the facial features are often only roughly sketched in and eyes, mouth, nose and moustache only indicated. The legs are either not in evidence at all, or only the tops of the thighs are to be seen. The figures were embedded in the tops of the mounds, and small areas containing sacrificial offerings signify what their function was.

Only stone statues from Scythian times are

so far known to have survived, but it is probable that the Scythians also carved figures from wood, an easier material to work on. We know from ancient sources that the eastern Scythians, the Sakas, raised a high mound to their dead queen Zarina, with a 'golden statue' on the top – possibly a gilded wooden figure.

In this brief survey we have attempted to convey an idea of the somewhat intractable, archaeologically assessable remains of the originally extensive cult areas represented by these necropoles. The visual effect, the ritual aura and power of attraction of such a cult area in its actual function was certainly far greater than we can imagine today, even if some recent important excavations have extended our knowledge of the subject.

The excavation findings from relatively remote regions of Kazakhstan and Tuva are of particular importance, where the burial mounds have been impaired only by the ravages of time and not by any human agency.

# 3 At the eastern end of the Scythian world

## Laid to rest on horses' tails

In the small village of Aržan in the river valley of the Uyuk, a particularly massive burial mound of a most unusual shape was for many years a source of considerable interest. It was known to the native people as *Aržan* (sacred, healing spring) or *Ulug-chorum* (massive kurgan). Aržan is situated in the centre of the Turanian-Uyukian steppe basin in the autonomous Soviet republic of Tuva, about 62 miles (100 km) from its capital, Kyzyl, and is the largest burial mound in the whole of the region. For stock-breeding nomads throughout the ages, this remote steppe basin and especially the Uyuk valley with its convenient, lush pastureland must have been a true haven. In winter the marsh flats covered in tall grass provide cattle with ample feed, while surrounding mountain steppes, below the snowline, offer plenty of rich grazing for sheep and horses, so that these animals hardly need further looking after. These exceptionally favourable climatic conditions attracted stock-breeding nomads for several thousand years, inducing tribal chiefs to set up their winter camps here. So it is no coincidence that in this sheltered area there is a considerable concentration of burial mounds, for the most part set out in lines.

The most striking aspect of the Aržan kurgan, apart from its enormous size (it has a diameter of 361 ft (110 m)), was its exterior form – a huge, round, stone-covered platform 10–13 ft (3–4 m) high with vertical stone walls. Until twenty years ago its total surface consisted of blocks of stone of 44–110 pounds (20–50 kilos) in weight. It is one of the great losses to archaeology that during the course of modern construction works this stone platform was removed and the inner area ploughed through by bulldozers. This caused an abrupt change in the conditions for preservation inside the huge complex, for owing to its temperature-reducing properties the protective stone covering had produced a microclimate in the core of the mound, isolated from the rest of the environment by a layer of ice, whose preserving effect had now been destroyed. If the archaeologists had arrived a few years earlier there would have been another treasure trove of organic material such as the astounding finds in the frozen tombs of Pazyryk. Even so, the scientific yield is sensational enough.

After four years' work, the two excavators M.P. Griaznov and M.Ch. Mannai-ool and their team have uncovered a tomb which is so far absolutely unique. The publication of their findings is eagerly awaited by experts in the field. Until now only brief interim reports have been available, which will be summarized here and supplemented by notes of conversations with the excavators at lectures and conferences. The western reader will thus gain an insight into these latest important excavations on the eastern edge of the Scythian world.

As mentioned above, the appearance of the Aržan kurgan was originally that of a flat, round stone tower. It owes its name to the peculiar circumstance of a large bowl-shaped depression having formed at its centre, from whose midpoint a spring flowed over the steppe with a water level of 8 ft (2.5 m). Water is always a precious commodity in such an environment, but the water from this spring was well known for its particular purity and pleasant taste; chemical analyses have since shown that it was remarkably sweet. From ancient times this water was believed to possess healing properties, and the spring was regarded as sacred. For the native people, the kurgan was consequently used as a place for cult activities and celebrations. Every year about 500 people would meet there in July, some travelling long distances, for communal worship and great tribal festivals. On these occasions the platform on the kurgan was covered in tent-shaped erections of stone and brushwood. Shamans, lamas and local potentates organized the festivities, which included competitions, especially horse races with 30 to 100 competitors. The celebrations ended in a great festive feast with huge quantities of boiled mutton, cheese and a kind of milk brandy which the participants had brought with them.

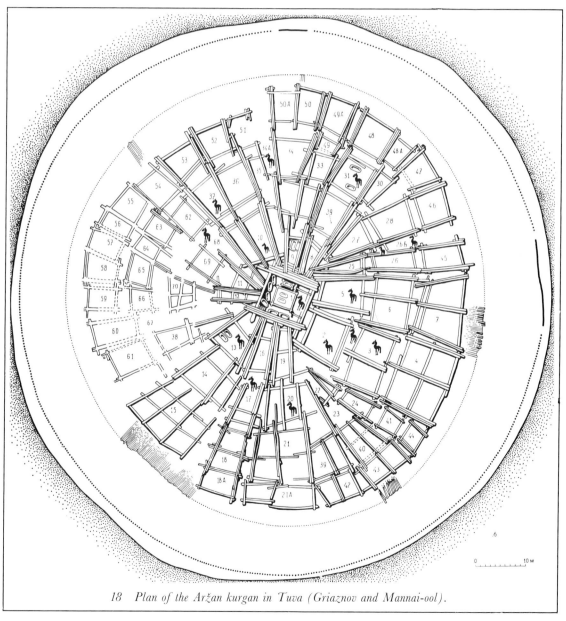

18   Plan of the Aržan kurgan in Tuva (Griaznov and Mannai-ool).

39

The excavation of this enormous burial mound lasted from 1971 to 1974. During this time the archaeologists uncovered a massive structure of a previously unknown type. It consists of an intricate complex of about seventy interlocking timber chambers which fill the whole of the inner area and surround – in circular formation – a very large chamber in the centre (see figs. 18 and 19).

Unfortunately this burial mound had also been thoroughly plundered by grave-robbers. They had penetrated down into the centre and from there had ransacked the individual chambers. However what remained, overlooked or lost by the robbers, still conveys a vivid idea of the original abundance of grave deposits. Taking first of all the central chamber (fig. 19), we find that it is 26 × 26 ft (8 × 8 m) square and encloses an inner chamber of about 13 × 13 ft (4 x 4 m) square with two wooden coffins and the burials of the 'king' and 'queen'. This inner chamber is

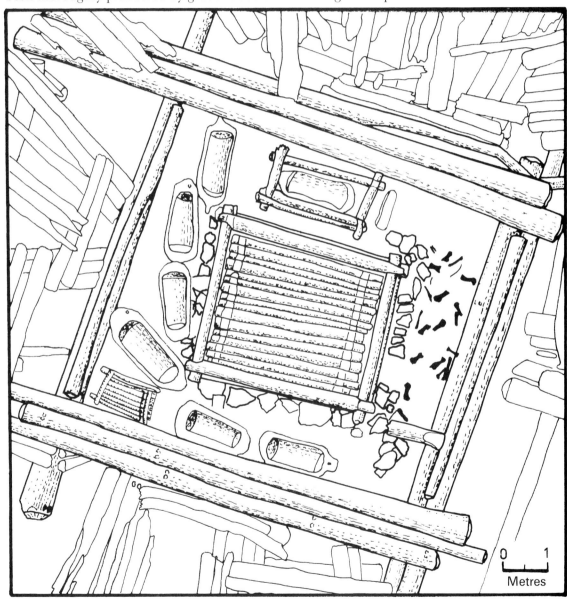

*19 Inner chamber of the Aržan kurgan (Griaznov and Mannai-ool).*

surrounded by six coffins resembling crude wooden troughs which were fashioned out of hollow tree trunks; in amongst these are two miniature wooden chambers. In these various receptacles the ruler's retainers were interred, ready to follow him into the next world. At the eastern end of the chamber lay his six favourite horses, together with the remains of their bridles which were decorated with gold. In spite of the wholesale plundering of the tomb, we can see from such typical finds as a golden neck ring, embossed gold plaques originally sewn on to garments, and fragments of turquoise inlay, that we are concerned here with the famous magnificent burial equipment of the nomad royalty of the time. The two bodies in the innermost chamber therefore doubtless wore gold-decorated clothing and precious jewellery similar to that worn by the young prince in the Issyk kurgan (see p. 47). Turquoise inlay of details in the heavy gold animal-art style plates is typical, as can be seen in the many examples preserved in the famous Siberian collection of Peter the Great, now in the Hermitage museum. Furs (including sable) and the remains of elaborately designed textiles, possibly imported, in three or four colours indicate that the original décor of the tomb must have been extremely colourful. It is to be hoped that by careful analysis during the scientific investigations, a reconstruction of the textile content of the grave can be undertaken so that we can discover details of the numerous carpets, wall-hangings and fur garments, etc.

In the other large chambers of this round wooden tower, as well as various clearly datable weapons, standards and the like, the skeletons of more than 150 horses were unearthed. The small horse symbol on the general plan indicates the places where the animals lay concentrated in large groups – often of 15–30 horses – frequently alongside the skeletons of 'horseherds' or 'equerries'. Many of the horses wore bridles, saddles or other adornment. A large bronze plate, 9.8 in (25 cm) in diameter, bearing the characteristic motif of the 'curled-up animal' (see fig. 20) – probably the breast armour and decoration of one of these horses – conveys a clear impression of the kind of opulent and elaborate equipment worn by the king's own favourite horses. Huge quantities of precious metal must have fallen into the hands of the robbers and been ruthlessly melted down.

The specific value of these modern investigations in the Far East lies in the numerous scientific analyses; these have produced a whole series of ritual details which it has never before been possible to observe with such precision. The sum of these details gives us an impressive picture of the material and indeed spiritual background of the whole complex inside the mound.

We shall consider first the difficult jigsaw puzzle necessary to solve the problem of the dating of the mound. The good condition of the timber made possible the application of dendrochronology. With this method of dating, the particular features of tree growth are used: owing to variations in temperature and rainfall, trees differ each year in their rate of growth. The rings seen in the cross-sections of the trunks are compared in the laboratory with those of other timber and where possible 'slotted in' to an existing standard chronology. In this way it is possible to identify matching periods of growth in timber found in different places. In the Soviet Union this method is gradually being applied geographically to the whole country, so that a comprehensive system can be evolved similar to that in central Europe which has already enjoyed a large measure of success, and which could one day make it possible to date timber to the exact year all over Europe. For the Siberian region we have to make do for the time being with relative dating, although even this is of great significance for the archaeologist. In the Aržan kurgan the numerous timber samples have revealed that all the tree trunks were felled at the same time, during the month of September. With the help of cross-dating from various dendrograms it was possible to link the Aržan kurgan with those of Pazyryk and Tuekta, about 311 miles (500 km) to the west. Therefore, although we cannot attempt absolute dating, we are in possession of relative information, according to which the timber for the Aržan kurgan must have been felled

241 years before that of the 5th Pazyryk kurgan. Nevertheless heated debate on the dating of the Aržan kurgan continues, although the differences in opinion vary only between the eighth and seventh or sixth centuries BC, a relatively short space of time.

Archaeological research on the Aržan kurgan has unearthed vital evidence concerning the power attributed to the dead ruler even after his death, and his economic power. One is struck first of all by the massive deployment of manpower, which can be best understood with the help of a reconstruction of the process of the building work:

The wooden 'round tower', flat at the top and about 10 ft (3 m) high and 262 ft (80 m) in diameter, together with its honeycomb of inner chambers has an area of roughly 54,000 sq ft (5000 sq m) and was built in a single session. The individual construction elements were fitted together in various operations so that a unified whole was created. The builders selected for their material more than 6000 trunks of 100-year-old larches from the nearby forest; these were dragged to the construction site, then the bark was removed and they were carefully smoothed down. The long, heavy trunks were then piled up loosely

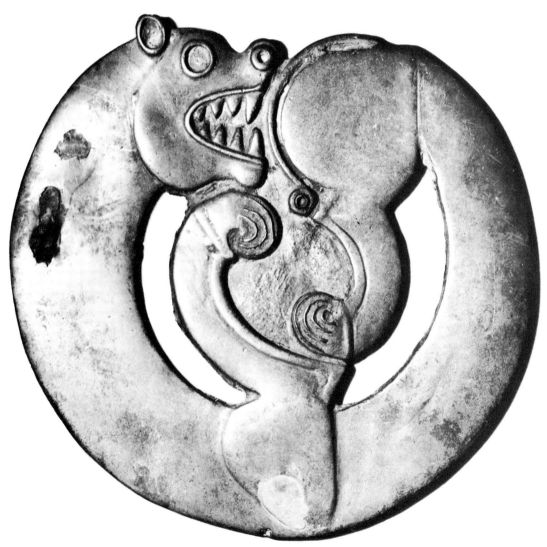

*20   Bronze curled animal from the Aržan kurgan, diameter 9.8 in. (25 cm) (Griaznov and Mannai-ool).*

or only lightly jointed on top of each other in such a way that they formed chambers up to 1600 sq ft (150 sq m) in area. Over the whole a timber ceiling was constructed, of a uniform thickness, and some chambers also had an extra ceiling. Access to the different sections was provided by passages between the separate chambers.

The excavators have calculated that 1200 people, well directed, could construct the complex in seven or eight days, assuming that twenty people with pack-horses could have been working at the same time on one timber chamber.

This huge complex, filled as it was with every conceivable artifact of everyday life, with over 150 horses – presumably brought in alive and then slaughtered – and surrounded by the crowd of participants in the funeral ceremonies of whom fifteen were killed as a retinue and placed in the various rooms, must have presented an overwhelming display of the wealth and power of its royal occupant. That is not all, however. The whole wooden structure was finally covered over with slabs of stone. Many thousands of slabs, each one so heavy that a full-grown man was needed to carry it, had to be dragged or carted to the site. In addition, a *krepis* was built round the foot of the mound – a surrounding stone wall approximately 8 ft (2.50 m) high.

As already shown by the Tolstaya mogila of Ordžonikidze, the latest excavations have given us an insight into an area of ritual which had previously seemed inaccessible from any practical point of view: namely, the funeral festivities which took place later. These involved at the very least a magnificent feast, at which hundreds, possibly thousands of people were present. The thorough excavation of these particular sections of the tomb revealed thousands of animal bones and pieces of smashed vessels from the remains of such festivities, amongst other things. The bones were carefully collected and painstakingly cleaned so that an osteological examination could be undertaken on the basis of which statistical evidence might be established. The field of archaeology owes certain vital information to such investigations: they, far more

than the impressive gold finds, have led to a realistic and graphic understanding of death and burial in the culture of the horse-riding nomads.

Round the foot of the Aržan kurgan, outside the wall, there was a large semicircular area designated for the depository of the remains of the funeral feast. In this cult area there were about 300 separate stone enclosures, each of 6–10 ft (2–3 m) in diameter, which contained selected bones (the skull and lower extremities) of cattle, sheep, goats and in particular horses. The skins of the animals which had been slaughtered and eaten in honour of the dead person were deposited here, in order to protect them from desecration. This ancient custom was very much alive in Siberia up until the 1920s. The skins of the slaughtered animals are hung for all to see, as proof that the rituals have taken place, and the skull and shinbones are retained within them. (Here we have the explanation of the fact that archaeologists always find these particular bones when excavating such places.) The calculations available so far for the Aržan have revealed that at least 300 horses were eaten at these memorial feasts. They need not of course all have been eaten at the same time.

On the surface of the mound a 'stag stone' was discovered. This is the term for large, elaborately decorated stone stelae which often depict stag motifs – though also stylized warriors and weapons of the time. In this case there is also a belt sculpted into the upper edge of the stone, with weapons hanging from it: a quiver, a dagger and a whetstone can be distinguished.

Much relating to the Aržan kurgan remains a mystery and invites further research: what is the significance of this strange and so far unique construction? Is it an imitation of an actual type of dwelling, or was it conceived only to meet the demands of the next world? What was it that occasioned the large number of sacrificial horses which were, according to the (still incomplete) examination of the bones, almost all 12–15-year-old stallions? This was certainly not a herd or *tabun*, since these consist for the most part of mares and

21 'Stag stone' with animal and weapon motifs from the Aržan kurgan (Griaznov and Mannai-ool).

young animals. Have we then here, as so often suggested, a final contribution from dependants to their master in the form of horses? The retainers who accompanied the 'king' into the next world were almost exclusively in the older age range: six of the men were over 60 and only one was between 18 and 20. Had these people grown old in the service of their master, and were they his closest retainers of perhaps high rank whom he wished to have around him in the next world too?

This is the highest number of human retainers that we know of so far discovered in one tomb in the Scythian world. As far as it is possible to tell, the 17 interred were all of the long-skulled Europid type. The ruler himself, as far as we can tell from the few surviving remains of his skeleton, was also very old, his bones showing changes characteristic of ageing. The sparse remains of a second skeleton seem to belong to an adult woman. Was this the 'queen' who followed her husband? Did the healing spring already exist, and had the dead man himself often visited this place so that he, like the later Mongol rulers, was buried in a place to which he had been particularly attached in his lifetime?

Owing to its special features, the burial mound with the healing spring at the most easterly edge of the Scythian world as we know it, goes beyond our previous notions of that culture and sets up new evidence for interpretation. A final example may reveal much about the mentality of the people who erected this immense structure: the timber-panelled floor of the innermost chamber containing the bodies of the 'king' and 'queen' did not rest directly on the steppe ground. In the space between, originally 7–8 in. (18–20 cm) deep, a considerable number of tail vertebrae were discovered which must have come from at least 15 or 20 horses' tails. The two 'royal' dead were literally laid to rest upon horsehair.

## The last council meeting

Large as the number of sacrificial horses in the Aržan kurgan may seem, a discovery as early as the last century shows that we must deal with numbers on quite a different scale.

In 1898 a burial mound 49 ft (15 m) high at Aul Ul' (or Ul'ski Aul), in the northern region of the Caucasus not far from Maikop, was excavated by the Russian archaeologist N.I. Veselovski. The method used was unfortunately that prevalent at the time. The excavator was content to dig a trench 82 ft

(25 m) wide and 197 ft (60 m) long into the centre. During this process he came across several skilfully positioned shafts dug by grave-robbers and one huge shaft from above, which already indicated that the tomb at the centre had been robbed and substantially destroyed. At this point the excavator began to show less interest in the possible potential of the tomb. He did not check to see whether a later burial had taken place in the mound (which might easily have been overlooked by the grave-robbers), nor did he widen his trench – which considering the dimensions of the mound was rather small-scale – and investigate whether the tomb continued to the right and left. The scene which met his eyes on the level of the original surface was nevertheless impressive enough: wherever one looked there were slaughtered horses! The remains of 360 lay neatly arranged on both sides of wooden barriers or in a circle round thick vertical posts, 18 to a group. Pegs and notches in the posts indicate that the animals were tethered to them before being slaughtered. The posts and barriers themselves, although in different order, stood to the south and north of the square burial chamber whose outline can be distinguished in the centre. The skeletons of

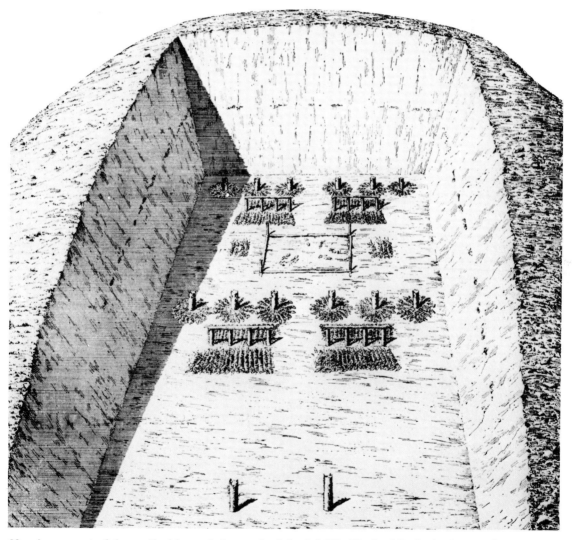

*22 Arrangement of the sacrificed horses in kurgan 1 of the Aul Ul' (Veselovski). In the foreground are two posts which probably marked the original entrance. They are 49 ft (15 m) from the first barrier.*

four head of cattle lay both to the east and to the west of the central chamber. Here also there were horse skeletons in large numbers; they had been disturbed by the grave-robbers, however, so that Veselovski did not establish their exact number, merely noting that the heads were all pointing towards the chamber. He also did not thoroughly check whether there was another elaborate skeleton formation to the east and west, similar to that to the north and south of the grave.

We therefore have to rely on guesswork. None of the animals was closely examined: their age, sex, height, coat colour and actual number are therefore unknown. The significance of the strict schematic arrangement is still a mystery. Veselovski's plan of the excavational finds gives the impression of some kind of camp. Two thick posts in the foreground, 17.5 ft (5.35 m) apart, form the entrance leading to the passageway between the first two barriers 49 ft (15 m) away. The distance between the rows of posts and the barriers is almost uniformly 14 ft (4.26 m) – the same distance as that between the barriers and the chamber.

There may have been such a well-ordered scene as this whenever the warriors appeared for a council with their leader and tethered their horses. What is surprising is that the animals were not bridled.

The grave in the centre had been so thoroughly plundered that we know virtually nothing about the potentate buried there. The remains of scale armour of bronze and iron, arrowheads, fragments of decorated gold foil, some bridles, pieces of two bronze cauldrons and a few shards of imported Greek pottery are all that have survived of the opulent burial equipment. We can however establish from these finds that the tomb dates from the sixth century BC. It is only the huge number of horses, so far unique in the whole of the Scythian region, together with the considerable height of the mound that convey an idea of the great power and wealth of the prince buried there. It is to be hoped that the kurgan, which has not yet been adequately excavated, will at some point be systematically and fully investigated. Amongst other things the excavators could clarify one of the great unsolved questions; namely that the elaborate ceremony of horse slaughtering, which must have taken place on the original steppe level, was to all appearances repeated when the mound had been raised to a third of its final height. In his report to the imperial archaeological commission in St Petersburg Veselovski writes that while digging through the mound he came across a layer of earth which had been stamped firm. He observed horse skeletons arranged in 'rows' and 'groups' over a fairly large area, which appeared to be tethered to posts. If we compare this with his plan of the lower structure, the parallel becomes clear. To the side of the groups of horses lay slaughtered cattle, donkeys and sheep.

After 50 skeletons the excavator stopped counting the horses on this upper level, but he noted quite positively that the layer with the skeletons continued through the side walls of his trench. We therefore do not know whether after a third of the mound was raised another platform was stamped firm and the ceremony of the 'council meeting' in honour of the dead tribal leader repeated, with more horses slaughtered, or whether a second burial of similar opulence took place on this level. Perhaps future archaeologists will find such a grave.

## The man with the golden helmet

If the Aržan kurgan and the mound of Ul'ski Aul have given an impressive picture of the extent of labour involved and of the slaughter of human beings and animals possible in Scythian times, a magnificent complex discovered in one of the cemeteries in Kazakhstan shows how the contents of the graves may have appeared before being plundered by grave-robbers.

During extensive systematic excavations in the burial-mound cemeteries of the Semireče (seven-river region) south of Lake Balkhash, archaeologists succeeded in uncovering a series of grave complexes which caused a great stir. In Semirečien there is a large concentration of kurgans, especially the high burial mounds of royalty. Until Issyk's sensational discovery in 1970, however, they all proved to have been robbed to such an extent that they could only be assigned to definite ethnic groups with difficulty.

The lavishness of the great burial mounds, however, their massive, well-preserved timber structures (see fig. 15) and the extensive sacrificial sites round the bases of the mounds, had attracted scholarly attention since the 1950s. It led to the idea which became prevalent in archaeological literature, that there must have been a huge grave area here too – similar to the Gerrhos of the European Scythians described by Herodotus – namely that of a large Sakan tribe. The Asiatic Scythians, the Sakas, were divided into several large tribes whose names we know for the most part from Persian sources. The most important to the east of the Caspian Sea were the *Saka haumavarga* (the 'hauma-drinking Sakas') and the *Saka tigraxauda* (the 'Sakas of the pointed caps' or 'pointed helmets'). Since the Persians won a glorious victory over the Sakas of the pointed caps in 520/19 BC under the leadership of their king, we have a large-scale relief portrayal of one such nomad king on the rockface of Bisutun (Iran) mentioned above. The Sakan king, Skuka, is depicted as the last in a long row of defeated 'lying kings' who stand bound before Darius. Skuka is portrayed as wearing the usual nomad dress – trousers and long, belted tunic. A striking feature is the tall pointed headdress which would normally have hung down to the shoulders but is here turned up and fastened with a band. The lower edge above the forehead appears to be decorated.

A headdress of this kind, magnificently worked with gold decoration and resembling a cap rather than a helmet, was discovered 31 miles (50 km) east of Alma-Ata in Issyk's necropolis, in the grave of a young man who had been buried, not in the great central grave with the 20 ft (6 m) high mound (which had been almost completely destroyed by grave-robbers), but in a relatively modest small wooden chamber to the side of the southern half. The robbers had overlooked his grave, and his costume and jewellery remained intact.

A predilection for glittering gold clothing is an essential characteristic of Scythian taste – with the men as well as the women of the ruling class. The numerous remains of golden adornments in the richer graves give the impression that the Scythians wished literally to 'gild' their dead. Gold seems to have exerted a magical power of attraction over the Scythians and – as we now know – over the Sakas as well, in all its various possibilities of application. The body of the man in the Issyk kurgan, 5 ft 4 in. (1.65 m) tall, was literally studded with jewellery and more than 4000 plates and plaques of decorated gold. The dead man wore relatively tight trousers with spangled seams, and boots decorated with gold. His upper garment, a short leather tunic, had 2400 arrow-shaped gold plaques sewn on to it, almost like scale armour, and all the edges and the sleeves were decorated with larger plates in the shape of animal faces. Under this he wore a cloth shirt embroidered with spangles which were arranged in patterns on the sleeves, some of the sequins being quite minute. Heavy gold animal figures were attached to the belt from which hung a long and a short sword, both of which were richly gilded and encased in decorated sheaths. Round the neck of the body lay a close-fitting necklace, made from a gold neck ring wound round four times, with two lionheads attached. On his right hand were two heavy gold rings, one of which was his signet-ring with an unusual portrayal of a human head wearing a kind of feathered crown. Its appearance bears a strong resemblance to a prehistoric 'Red Indian', and had this object not come to light during a reliable modern excavation one would initially be tempted to regard it as a forgery. However, this burial complex – as well as the extraordinary signet – does date from the period of the fifth century BC.

The most impressive object found in the tomb was the pointed headdress. This was about 25.5 in. (65 cm) high, and the excavators were able to reconstruct it in exact detail. Round its lower edge is a magnificent diadem consisting of various elaborately intertwined

23  Plan of the grave in the Issyk kurgan. The timber chamber contained vessels of red earthenware, silver and bronze at the head end of the body, and flat wooden dishes and ladles were found at his right side. A bronze mirror lay on the left near the skull. The dead youth wore a sumptuous costume with an elaborate headdress and rich gold jewellery. He was also equipped with two magnificently ornamented swords and a whip bound in gold, with the handle resting close to his head. See p. 51 for a description of other deposits.

24  The excavator K.A. Akišev's reconstruction conveys a vivid picture of the dead youth (right).

25    The Sakan King Skuka is led bound before Darius (Hinz). The long neck shield of his pointed helmet is turned up and fastened at the top. The edges of this and those of the lower section of the helmet appear to be ornamented.

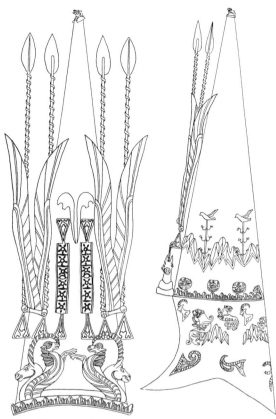

shafts decorated with spirals. The centre space between these is taken up with two elongated strips of gold foil painted in black and red. On the sides of the headdress, joining on to the ornamentation of the front, is the depiction of a landscape populated with animals which had been cut like silhouettes out of gold foil: winged tigers, snow leopards, ibex, birds and masks, all inhabiting 'golden mountains' and trees.

26 *The gold-trimmed headdress from the Issyk kurgan. On the point stood a small gold ram, possibly a mark of royalty (Akisev).*

27 *The gold signet ring from the right hand of the body, perhaps an attempt to depict his magnificent headdress (Akisev).*

fabulous animals which had been carved out of wood and then covered with a thin layer of gold leaf. This technique of gilding is typical of the eastern region, though it also occurs in the European part of Scythia. By this relatively simple device the animals were given the appearance of solid gold. Above the forehead the animals join together into a closed group. Two horned heads resembling those of mountain goats (bezoar goats?) and two front halves of kneeling horses are joined together by a winged body. In the space behind, the front halves of two more horses are seen rearing up, their hooves touching. Above this a number of gold-foil decorations in the form of wings or feathers ascend towards the top of the headdress, whose point is finished off by the miniscule statuette of a ram. Thrusting upwards out of these wings or feathers are four arrows or miniature spears with long

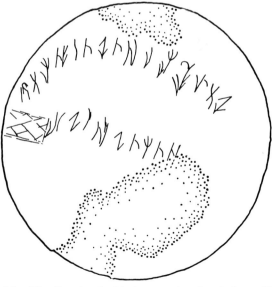

28 *The silver bowl with the mysterious inscription, still undeciphered, the oldest such find in central Asia (Akisev).*

# The home of the 'sharp-beaked, dumb dogs of Zeus'

The burial in the Issyk kurgan testifies to the gold riches of the Sakan country which lay not so far from what, according to ancient mythology, was the home of the 'gold-guarding griffons'. In Kazakhstan, as in the Altai immediately to the east, gold was mined from Bronze Age times (c. 1500 BC) at the very latest, in both opencast and underground mines. The first archaeological survey in 1941 listed 70 ancient goldmines in Kazakhstan alone, whose exploitation since the Bronze Age can be traced.

The whole of north Kazakhstan emerges as one huge quarry, especially the area around Stepnyak, Maykain and Bestyube (north of Karaganda). A substantial number of ancient mining sites with datable tools, such as stone mallets, pick-axes, wedges etc., enable us to make relatively precise deductions regarding the quarrying processes of antiquity. The miners used wooden climbing-posts for the descent and ascent. The vertical shafts reached a depth of up to 98 ft (30 m), and great care was taken to remain above ground water-level or at least to descend only minimally below it, no doubt to avoid the risk of water penetration. It seems that the miners of antiquity worked in the shafts and tunnels without the benefit of wooden struts and props.

As yet no thorough scientific investigation has been undertaken of the ancient mines of Siberia and central Asia. Most of them are in fact being reworked, and the old traces have been destroyed or filled in during modern quarrying. Productive mining sites have often been rediscovered with the help of ancient folk tradition, frequently also on the basis of old place-names meaning 'gold' or through general indications of the whereabouts of shafts, pits or quarries.

The rich gold deposits of Kazakhstan, found in the 1920s after a careful search based on just such folk tradition, were almost all *re*-discovered. They had already been exploited since the Bronze Age, and were later forgotten. Present-day mining has frequently unearthed traces of the ancient mine-workers, who had tunnelled horizontally as well as in descending inclines. Cavities of more than 197 ft (60 m) in length and 46 ft (14 m) wide, with a height of 2.6 ft (0.80 m) supported by layers of stone left standing, convey an approximate idea of the extent of prehistoric mining. As well as such large working areas, conspicuously small ones were also discovered which are very narrow and never more than a few metres long – probably the working places of children or adolescents.

The object of prehistoric mining was always to discover veins with a high gold content. The composition of the waste heaps shows that only the larger grains of gold and nuggets were extracted, the remainder going to waste. With the aid of modern purification plants the ancient waste heaps are therefore also being industrially processed; in one place for example several hundred thousand tons of old waste were found to have a gold content. Reports of such quantities, and descriptions of large waste heaps on which it was possible for a forest of century-old trees to grow, testify both to the considerable passage of time and to the enormous extent of the goldmining in antiquity.

After its extraction the ore containing the gold was taken to be processed at sites which have also been established, where it was broken into small pieces and washed. The sites are usually near ancient lakes, and are sometimes as large as half a kilometre square. Great numbers of implements are found here – mortars, slabs, stone pestles, axes, sledge-hammers and knapping hammers which were used to crush and grind to powder the quartz ore which contained the gold. Part of the ore brought to the processing sites seems to have been left unprocessed, for reasons not known.

Similarly, clear evidence of goldmining can be found in the Altai, immediately to the east, which owes its name ('mountains of gold') to its rich deposits. Here in Zmeinogorska (snake mountain) an ancient miner who had met with a fatal accident was discovered. Next to his skeleton, which was permeated with metal oxide, a leather bag still lay, well filled with gold minerals.

It was into these regions, where according

to ancient mythology the 'gold-guarding griffons' worked their mischief – the 'sharp-beaked, dumb dogs of Zeus' as Aeschylus calls them in his *Prometheus* (803), where the dreaded mounted army of the one-eyed Arimaspians (*arima* being the Scythian word for 'one' and *spu* for 'eye', Herodotus IV, 28) was said to live by a river that flowed over gold, and where, finally, 'gold-digging ants' had been introduced – it was into these ancient goldmining regions that a caravan route led.

We learn from Herodotus that this route stretched from the Greek city of Olbia through Scythia and far into the Asian interior. It was used by Greeks and Scythians to conduct their trade. The Scythians, it was reported, had to employ seven interpreters to communicate with the various peoples on this long route. Although the subject of the negotiations and the reason why this almost endless route was deemed to be worth travelling are not mentioned in the ancient source, we can guess what they were.

There are no gold deposits in the Ukraine. All the Scythian gold jewellery found there which we admire so much today was fashioned from imported gold. The gold – the spoils of war and tribute apart – had to be paid for, which gives us an indication of the Scythians' enormous economic power.

There has as yet been no analysis in the Soviet Union of the gold with which archaeologists are concerned, so that we can give no information regarding its origin and chemical composition. There are, however, in principle only three areas from which Scythian gold could have originated: Transylvania in the west, where gold had been extracted through mining and the panning of river sand since ancient times (it was here that the Agathyrsi settled, a tribe related to the Scythians, whose love of rich gold jewellery is mentioned in ancient sources). The second area was the Caucasus, especially Colchis, home of Medea, where the legend of the Golden Fleece originated. This legend touches on an ancient method of collecting gold: deposits were panned from river sand and directed along artificial channels, and the gold-dust was deposited on sheepskins which thus became 'golden' fleeces. It is very probable that the third area of origin was Kazakhstan and the Altai Mountains.

It is against this background that the purpose of the mysterious caravan route becomes clear. Owing to a considerable amount of further evidence, its existence can now also be verified archaeologically.

The mounted warriors of the one-eyed Arimaspian tribe would rob the griffons of their gold and take possession of it themselves, according to ancient legend.

With this brief survey of the great mining centres of the Asian interior we have attempted to throw some light on the reality behind these mysterious myths.

The clothing and jewellery of the dead youth in the Issyk kurgan clearly reflect the ruling class's familiarity with gold, of which there were such abundant supplies and to which they were so accustomed that they even found it necessary to add red and black touches of paint in order to increase its visual attraction.

# 4 What were they like?

## Physical appearance and dress

Herodotus does not describe the physical characteristics of the Scythians in Book IV, although it does seem from the general tone of his account that he did not find their appearance particularly objectionable. His frequent meetings with Scythians and Persians, coupled with the fact that he himself was a native of Asia Minor, may have contributed to his tolerant attitude. He was even dubbed a 'barbarian-lover' after his frank and undistorted description of the non-Greek peoples during his public lectures in Athens.

Another famous traveller describes the Scythians' physical appearance in much more detail. Following the normal convention we shall refer to this unknown writer as Pseudo-Hippocrates, a name which derives from the fact that his *Treatise* ('De aere, aquis, locis') was included in the *Corpus Hippocraticum*. This author was a doctor in the second half of the fifth century BC and was evidently much travelled. Apart from the Greek regions and Egypt, he was also familiar with the Caucasus and Maeotis (the area around the present-day Sea of Azov). Finding the climate uncongenial in the extreme, this visitor to the north Pontic steppes first of all gives a concise account of the conditions under which the inhabitants lived. He then goes on to describe what is, in his view, the deplorable state of the natives' health – that of the Scythians in particular. And it certainly sounds bad enough: the Scythians were small, he writes, plagued with arthritis, the women practically sterile.... Their bodies were damp and sweaty (this could only be relieved to some extent by blood-letting) and flabby, and they were bow-legged and dumpy. Because of the constant cold their skin was a reddish colour; he finds the Scythian women particularly repellent – and they were fat into the bargain. He goes on to say that their life on horseback caused swelling of the vertebrae and hip problems, even rendering the men impotent (which he sees, together with the obesity of the women, as the reason for the apparently low birth rate). Altogether the wretched climate, constant life on horseback and what he considered the harmful wearing of trousers (making it impossible for the men to keep fondling themselves) were in his opinion the three basic evils of the Scythian way of life. They were responsible for the numerous ills which beset the Scythians, he maintains, laying particular stress on the impossibility of regular sexual intercourse. Owing to their life on horseback the Scythian nobility were at an extreme disadvantage.

One can feel sorry for this poor traveller who must have had a hard time of it on his journeys. It is not only that he describes the climate of present-day Ukraine and its coastal strip with the subtropical Crimea (to us a fairly reasonable climate) as if it were Siberia – this is quite common for the Graeco-Roman world. But the natives also, with their way of life diametrically opposed to his – their horse-riding in particular which he personally found so loathsome – must have been absolutely repellent to him. His unappetizing portrayal of their stature, skin colour and other physical attributes was distorted by his alien sensitivities. It nevertheless has an air of scholarly

54

objectivity, and led to completely erroneous conclusions regarding this physical type. Right up to the present century it has been assumed that the Scythians were a Mongol people (cf. A. Blok's famous poem); apart from a reddish (or yellowish) skin colour and obesity, the author also attributes to them, among other things, the absence of beard growth. Research and a number of newly discovered accounts of the Scythians have in the meantime confirmed that we are dealing here with an extremely biased account, saturated with personal aversions, which was at best only accurate when describing exceptions.

Anthropological information available to us so far indicates that the Scythians were relatively tall. This tallness is particular noticeable in warrior burials and those of men of the upper social stratum, who would seem tall even today. They are often over 6 ft (1.80 m) in height, sometimes over 6 ft 3 in. (1.90 m), and have occasionally even been

29　*The faces of the two main figures on the gold pectoral of Ordžonikidze, Rayon Nikopol'. For the whole pectoral see colour plate 14 (Photo: Kločko). The artist gave the man on the left a concentrated, almost painful expression, and the one on the right ringlets, probably in imitation of the Greek fashion.*

known to exceed 6 ft 6 in. (2 m). There is a substantial difference in height between members of the upper social stratum and the ordinary people of, on average, 4–6 in. (10–15 cm). Where men are concerned, height can thus without doubt be interpreted as a mark of social status. This phenomenon can be observed all the way to the eastern extremity of the Scythian world. In the Altai graves all those interred who were from the upper social stratum can be distinguished by their height and powerful bodies. All these men are between 5 ft 8 in. (1.76 m) and 6 ft (1.80 m) tall; the men in the common graves are on average 5 ft 4 in. (1.64 m) tall. Anthropological research has established that these skeletons differ from those of today in their longer arm and leg bones and a generally stronger bone formation. In European Scythia, including the Caucasus regions, we are dealing with Europids in Scythian times who betray no Mongol characteristics but who do divide into long- and round-skulled types.

The physical characteristics of the Scythians correspond to their cultural affiliation: their origins place them within the group of Iranian peoples. According to traditional myths and legends, and also to various archaeological findings, they arrived from the east or the south-east in the region north of the Black Sea and intermarried with the autochthonous peoples, presumably mainly with the native Cimmerians who had settled in the region before them. The language of the Scythians is closely related to that of the ancient Ossetes (the remainder of the Ossetes tribe today live in the Terek region of the north Caucasus).

Further east, the Mongol characteristics of the skulls of the indigenous Sauromatian peoples become more apparent. Nevertheless we must remember that we are dealing with a period in which huge areas of Siberia far into Mongolia were still inhabited by ancient Europids. It was only gradually – in the first millennium BC – that Mongol characteristics became apparent in this area, characteristics which are today almost universal in that region; at the same time the fifth or fourth century must have represented a certain turning point. The seventeen burials in the Aržan kurgan, for instance, which definitely originate from the eighth to the sixth century BC, are, as far as can be ascertained, of the long-skulled Europid type. In the Pazyryk kurgans, however, which originate from the fifth to the third century, the men are of very mixed physical characteristics while the women still show definite Europid features. A particularly interesting 'mixed marriage' was discovered in kurgan 2. The man interred here, who will be discussed in more detail below – he is tattooed and scalped – was at first sight clearly of Mongol appearance. This can be seen in the shape of the head and the face with its prominent cheekbones, and the rather coarse, black hair. But there were traces of stubble a few days old on his chin, so he must have had beard growth which is not a Mongol characteristic. The woman buried with him, who was over forty, had by contrast a longish face and was also in other respects quite different in type from the man. On examination it was found that both must have suffered from severe toothache while they were alive – in the woman's case caused by suppuration of the gums.

If the upper social element of the Altai population is compared with the burials in the simple graves, it is noticeable that there is a considerable proportion of Europids among the lower social stratum. Rudenko, the excavator of the Altai kurgans, has interpreted this phenomenon in the light of tribal aristocracies, derived from the field of ethnology. It is his theory that physically contrasting types are likely to be encountered in aristocratic families, since vast distances were involved where exogamy was prevalent. This cannot, however, be the only reason for the racial differences which only emerge at a relatively late date and are furthermore so immediately obvious. They doubtless have to be considered against a background of political displacement and other cultural and personal contact.

Owing, possibly, to the great caravan route to the east, knowledge of this racial mixing had also reached the Greek settlements on the Black Sea. Herodotus already knew of it and reports (IV, 23) that beyond the various tribes

30 *Head of the man from the 2nd Pazyryk kurgan (Rudenko).*

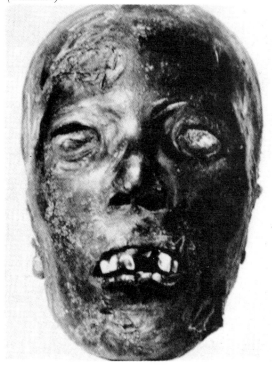

31 *Head of the woman from the 2nd Pazyryk kurgan (Rudenko).*

of the Asiatic Scythians over to the east, bald-headed people lived in the foothills of a high mountain chain. 'Their noses are said to be flat and their chins broad. They have their own language but dress in the Scythian fashion', he writes, repeating the rumours. It is possible that here he is describing the Pazyrykans, or at any rate their immediate neighbours.

## 'Bodies clothed in skins, with curly hair'[8]

Returning to the European Scythians, we find that a wealth of representations provides us with a fairly vivid picture of their appearance.

In 1969 a team led by the Kiev archaeologist V.I. Bidzilya, investigating the massive Gaymanova mogila burial mound and its various underground catacomb graves in two summer digs, came across a magnificent set of drinking vessels which had been cleverly hidden in a side grave at the head end of the body. After archaeologists had painstakingly uncovered the carefully stacked bowls of gold and silver, they discovered at the bottom of this unique 'safe' a hemispherical silver bowl with handles. The outer wall was decorated with an embossed gilt pictorial frieze, and this vivid representation caused immediate jubilation in the scientists present.

Altogether there are six figures in the composition on this vessel: two on the front, two on the back, and one under each handle at the sides. Unfortunately only the front side is in a good state of preservation, the back being in rather poor condition. The extremely graphic scene on the front depicts two older warriors comfortably engrossed in conversation. Their heads, turned towards each other, are effectively highlighted by the contrast between the gold of their hair and beards and the silver of their broad faces. Their slightly open mouths and the faraway look in their eyes also enhances the lifelike impression. From their whole appearance it is clear that venerable leaders of equal rank are portrayed here. This is confirmed by the magnificently embellished weapons and the signs of honour, which we know from literature, that they hold almost playfully in their raised hands: the one on the left is holding a whip, and the one on the right a club-shaped sceptre. The two warriors on the back of the vessel also seem engaged in lively discussion. They seem younger and more wiry – the one on the left at least, as far as we can tell from the portrayal. To the right and left of them a servant or retainer is kneeling and serving the two men. The one on the right, an older, sedate man, is touching his forehead in a gesture of respect and seems about to serve them with a bird, perhaps a goose, shown next to him. The one on the left, who from his lack of beard and his appearance in general seems still a youth, has brought in a sack or leather bag which could contain a refill, perhaps *koumiss* (fermented mare's milk), for the two main figures (see below).

They are all wearing typical Scythian dress, though splendidly fashioned and with the particularly fine addition of long, pointed flaps all round, which must have waved up and down very effectively when they were on horseback. The long braided tunics are of embroidered, fur-trimmed leather. Trousers, embroidered lengthways, and soft ankle-length boots complete their outfit.

This then was the national costume of the Scythians. Ovid, coming into contact with variants of it in Tomis, his place of exile on the western border of the steppes, describes it with distaste: 'They wear skins and stitched trousers as protection from the cold, and the only part of their body one sees is their face.' To Roman eyes, especially in combination with the strong smell of leather and possible lack of cleanliness, this must indeed have been

a repulsive sight.

On the other hand archaeological evidence shows fairly conclusively that this riding costume was in fact smart, costly and splendidly fashioned. Different kinds of leather and fur were cleverly combined for comfort and effect on horseback, and many sorts of magnificent coloured embroidery and appliqué work are evident in complicated patterns and figures, often with lavish facings of pearl and gold.

If we look at the stature of the hero on the left-hand side at the front of the bowl, and at his paunch, so faithfully reproduced by the artist, we can see why such figures would seem 'bloated' and 'sweaty' to the writer in the Hippocratic *Treatise*, and why he could not tell where their joints were; they hardly correspond to the Greek ideal of beauty, it is true.

One can well believe, however, that these portly figures with their air of self-confidence and strength were capable of the vigorous utterances attributed to Scythian leaders:

'Persian, such is my nature: I have never yet fled from any man in fear, nor am I fleeing now from you.... But you will yet weep bitter tears for having claimed to be my master.' (Reply from the Scythian King Idanthyrsus to Darius, who was demanding the former's submission; Herodotus IV, 127.)

'... return home, happy and free and grateful to the gods and the Scythians! But we will so deal with your former master that he will never again launch a campaign against any other nation.' (Message to the Ionians during the pursuit of the fleeing Darius which almost ended in catastrophe for the latter; Herodotus IV, 136).

*32a   Gold-plated silver bowl from the Gaymanova mogila, second half of the fourth century BC (Bidzilya). The bowl, 4 × 3.8 in. (10.5 × 9.7 cm) in size, stood in a hiding-place buried in the floor of the grave which contained only costly drinking vessels (see p. 113).*

*32b   The flattened-out version of the whole depiction showing the portrayal of six figures. Sheep heads are fixed to the side handles, and the base is decorated with geometric designs.*

*33   Detail on the bowl from the Gaymanova mogila. The left of the two elderly leaders with goryt and whip, his left arm leaning on his shield.*

In contrast to present-day ideas, trousers were to the Greeks an article of female attire, the legend being that they were invented by a woman. Diodorus writes (Book 2, Ch. 6) that the clever and beautiful Semiramis, summoned by her husband to his military camp so that he could make love to her, devised for the arduous and dangerous journey the practical trouser costume which would conceal its wearer's sex. These trousers, combined with a jacket or wrap, were adequate for all requirements, protecting the skin from the heat on the long journey and allowing freedom of movement in any activity. Indeed the garment could be so handsomely fashioned that both the horse-riding warriors of Eurasia and the Medes and Persians kept to this 'Semiramis costume' and knew how to wear it with elegance.

As yet we know less about the dress of the women of the region north of the Black Sea than that of the men. New finds seem to be closing this gap, however, although a complete reconstruction still presents difficulties since women were far less often depicted than men – certainly not in any precise detail.

Conditions in the graves for the preservation of textiles, felt, leather and similar organic materials were generally very poor. Only traces of colour and a very few remains of thread on the uncovered skeletons indicate the original colourful clothing. An important aid to the reconstruction of the female attire of the nobility is the lavish gold ornamentation which adorned the sleeves, upper garment, various hems and edges and even the shoes. With the help of such ornamentation the contours of the different garments can frequently be clearly traced. The women of the upper social echelons wore long robes – at least on certain ceremonial occasions – possibly with furbelows round the lower edge, and over these long, baggy, richly ornamented coats. Shoes or short boots with gold decoration could be seen under these long garments, as the grave finds show. On their heads they wore magnificent headdresses and obviously great store was set by the form of these, whether individual or according to fashion. They were sometimes like diadems with long flowing purple veils, sometimes close-fitting like a cap, and sometimes magnificent affairs over 12 in. (30 cm) high, glittering with gold. Some women had different kinds of headgear with them in the grave, presumably so that they would always be suitably dressed at the various ceremonies and during their representational duties in the next world.

Completing the appearance of the ladies,

34 Fourth-century BC gold plaque from the Melitopol' kurgan; size 1.3 × 1 in. (3.3 x 3 cm) (Photo; Kločko).

35 Artist's impression of a scene on the ceremonial headdress from the Karagodeuašh kurgan (Mancevič).

who were already laden with gold, was a huge amount of jewellery. Their fingers were adorned with rings of various shapes (sometimes ten or even more), round their wrists lay gold bangles and various bracelets of pearls and other material, and in addition they had solid gold neck rings, earrings and other jewellery. Unfortunately practically nothing so far is known about their hairstyles.

That they did not rely solely on nature but used artificial aids where necessary is shown by the remains of coloured make-up and other indications of the use of cosmetics. The delicate bottles and little bowls found at the head of the dead or in the care of a special servant, perhaps a 'chambermaid' killed for the burial, probably contained scented water and ointments. Bronze mirrors, hardly ever absent in the graves of lavishly-buried women (and also found in men's graves), were doubtless intended in their polished state to reflect the idealized image of the sumptuously dressed women against a golden background of warm, flattering light.

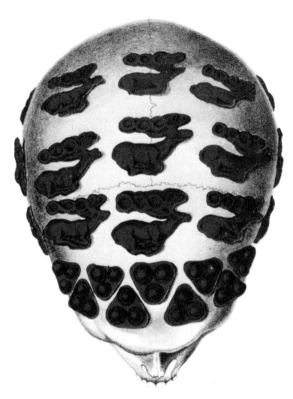

36 Sinyavka, kurgan 100. Gold decoration of a cap on the skull of the main burial. Sixth century BC (Bobrinskoi).

## The custom of blood-brotherhood

By drinking a mixture of wine and their own blood, in which their swords, arrows, axes and spears had previously been dipped and over which long incantations had been murmured, two warriors used to swear their allegiance to each other to the death. We know from literature of extremely moving stories of such blood brothers and their close bonds which in the dangers of daily life were doubtless of immense importance. The sacrifice of property, wife and children, eyesight and one's life, together with the unconditional pledge to fight for one's blood brother, were an essential component of Scythian ideals and glorified accordingly. Lucian, an author of the second century BC, who felt to some extent akin to the Scythians because of his non-Greek (Syrian) origins, has the Scythian Toxaris tell five dramatic stories on this subject in his narrative *Toxaris, or the Friends*.

As well as the written accounts, numerous depictions show details of this warriors' cus-

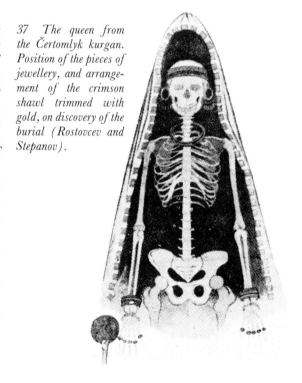

37 The queen from the Čertomlyk kurgan. Position of the pieces of jewellery, and arrangement of the crimson shawl trimmed with gold, on discovery of the burial (Rostovcev and Stepanov).

61

tom. The ceremony of the drink itself is shown, as well as the advantages of such a bond in battle, where the protagonists are always shown as equal in rank – doubtless an important factor where a bond to the death is concerned.

In spite of the relatively short time since its discovery, a whole series of interpretations of the main scene on the Gaymanova bowl has already been put forward. We like to see in it an idealized representation of renowned warriors closely bound to each other, perhaps a Scythian variant of the famous musketeers of Alexandre Dumas.

What is not particularly stressed in written accounts, but becomes clear in pictorial representations of drinking ceremonies, is the fact that on this solemn occasion the two warriors drank from a single vessel – a drinking horn or similar. The two future blood brothers mixed wine with their blood, leant close together and drank the mixture, both lifting the vessel up to their lips. The simultaneous drinking was obviously important; it sealed the bond to the death and perhaps even beyond into the next world. The ceremony was witnessed by the noblest warriors of the surrounding area.

38   *Gold plaque with scene of blood-brotherhood from the Kul'-Oba-kurgan, in the Crimea. Height 2 in. (4.9 cm). Fourth century BC.*

This well-established ritual ceremony has helped archaeologists to expose a series of modern forgeries of Scythian pictorial work, since the custom of blood-brotherhood among Scythian warriors, so vividly described in written sources, proved a favourite subject with forgers. They overlooked the essential element of drinking together from one vessel, however, so that on the modern 'works of antiquity' the blood brothers are either drinking simultaneously from two cups or one after the other from a vessel held by both.

This mistake in motif is an important clue to forgeries which are otherwise so expertly crafted that they can deceive even the specialists. The south Russian forgers around the turn of the century posed the biggest threat, because of their excellent craftsmanship and the extremely high quality of their work. Every new Scythian treasure to emerge from the obscurity of the tombs served the forgers as a model. The objects were copied, their form changed, they were translated into a different context – and put on the market. Herodotus's Book IV, whose detailed descriptions acted as a stimulus, was literally 'cannibalized'. It was the large museums of western Europe which suffered the most. The director of the Odessa museum, Ernst von Stern, waged a bitter war against these forgers. At the tenth Archaeological Congress in 1896 he emerged into the public eye with his lecture, 'Forgeries in the Odessa museum and forgers' activities in south Russia'.

Probably the most notorious scandal involving a forgery from southern Russia concerned an extremely costly purchase by the Louvre. This was the 'Tiara of Saitapharnes' which – as subsequently proved – had in fact been made by the Odessa goldsmith I. Ruchumovski. This magnificent headdress was at first interpreted by experts of the time as archaeological verification of an episode known to us from a famous Greek inscription – the 'Protogenes Decree'. This stone inscription expressed the gratitude of the citizens of Olbia to one of their number, and originates from around the end of the third or beginning of the second century BC. In it the rich Protogenes is warmly praised for his frequent gifts of money to the city. The Protogenes Decree is of particular importance to archaeology, as it describes the state of the Greek city colony of Olbia, by then impoverished, in a period which otherwise remains obscure to a large extent, and for which there are scarcely any archaeological sources. We are told of the threatening behaviour of the barbarian King Saitapharnes, who appeared outside the city and had to be propitiated with costly gifts. Unfortunately the surviving text of the Protogenes inscription breaks off at the point where Protogenes and Aristocrates have brought gifts to Saitapharnes, which he does accept but which nevertheless anger him. The tiara, which was thought to have been wrought to suit the ornate taste of a nomad king, seemed to fit the historical context admirably. The skilful forger had even thought of putting an inscription on the tiara itself, which read: 'The council and citizens of Olbia honour the great and invincible King Saitapharnes.'

The exposure of the forgery caused a huge scandal, but the tiara was soon forgotten, and is now shamefacedly hidden somewhere in the Louvre, though its creator's craftsmanship in fact deserves a certain amount of recognition.

# 5  Armed warriors on red steeds

## Weapons and fighting methods

Although modern studies of weapons and fighting methods are far from complete, the countless individual finds of weapons and whole sets of fighting equipment already indicate, after their systematic restoration, a completely new picture of fighting methods and have significantly contributed to a new evaluation of the Scythians. Today it is possible to give a description of the function of the weapons and of fighting techniques, as well as a sound estimation of the overall picture, including necessary statistics. It turned out to be very favourable for archaeology that Scythian funeral rites stipulated the burial of an abundance of weapons with the dead. Despite looting by grave-robbers throughout the ages, enough objects of weaponry have survived to make possible a reconstruction of the fighting methods of these ancient mounted warriors – although what remains is of course only a fraction of the original material. Even with this limitation it has nevertheless been established that no other people in history have provided archaeologists with so many objects of weaponry as have the Scythians.

Just as he would ride into battle in life, a dead Scythian also went into the next world laden with weapons, no doubt expecting battle tournaments and all sorts of military activity there. Literally armed to the teeth, and provided with spare equipment as well, the interred warriors present a remarkably vivid reflection of their everyday life.

In written sources the Scythians appear as the equals of their various enemies, among which were the Assyrian, Persian and Greek armies. The abundance of archaeological deposits discovered since shows the material basis for this and also clearly indicates that they could assimilate innovatory weapon technology, adapting it to their own needs, in a relatively short time.

The variety and sophistication of their weaponry of attack and defence is astounding, and must have caused their enemies severe problems. Among the weapons of attack the bow and arrow took first place. These are also present even in the commonest graves, which explains why the Scythians are referred to in ancient sources as a people of mounted archers. Arrow production reached enormous proportions, and in the graves whole magazines of arrows are found with hundreds,

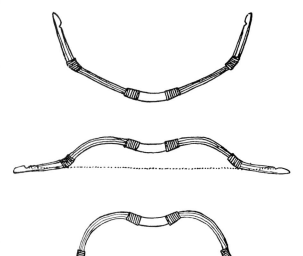

*39  Composite bow unstrung, strung and ready to shoot ( Mitscha-Märheim).*

1  The Nečaeva mogila, the highest Scythian kurgan of the north Pontic steppe still in existence.

2  The rolling forest steppe in the district of Smela. This type of landscape merges into the Pontic steppe in the north and extends over vast stretches of Russia.

**Horse no. 5**          **3–6  The sacrificed horses from the 1st Pazyryk kurgan.**

**Reconstruction of trappings, mane and tail decoration, and adornments (after Griaznov) by Herz and Rolle.**

Horse no. 10

**Horse no. 6**

**Horse no. 7**

**Horse no. 8**

**Horse no. 1**

**Horse no. 3**

**Horse no. 2**

**Horse no. 4**

**Horse no. 9**

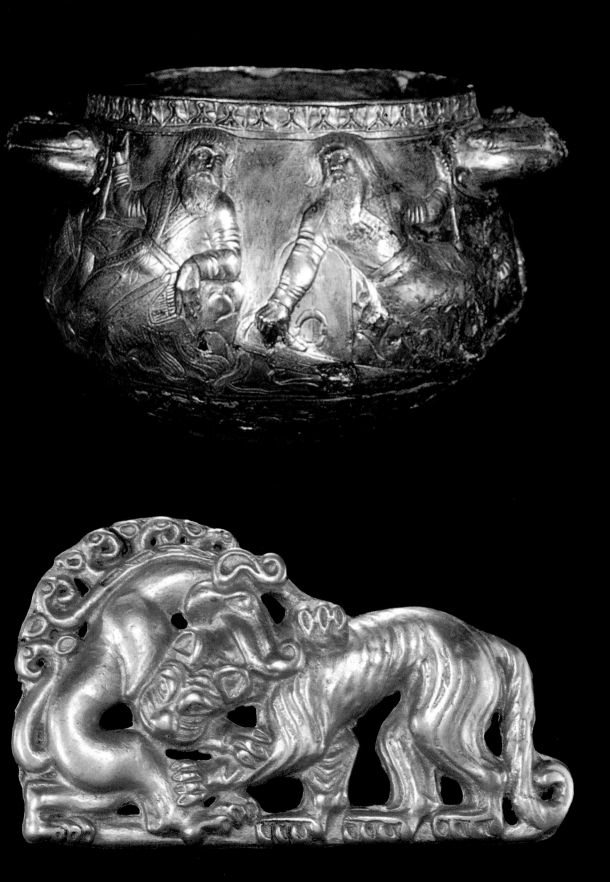

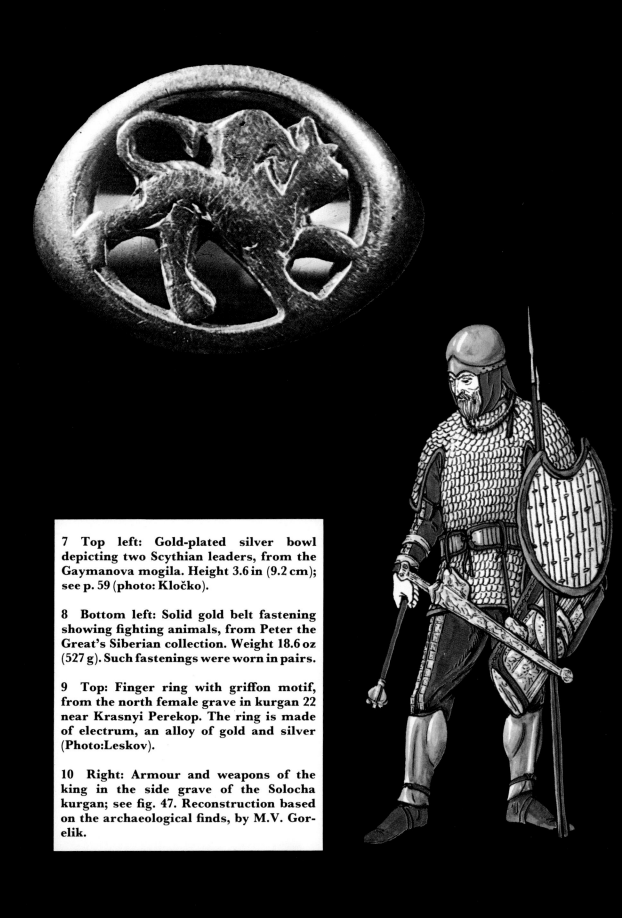

7 Top left: Gold-plated silver bowl depicting two Scythian leaders, from the Gaymanova mogila. Height 3.6 in (9.2 cm); see p. 59 (photo: Kločko).

8 Bottom left: Solid gold belt fastening showing fighting animals, from Peter the Great's Siberian collection. Weight 18.6 oz (527 g). Such fastenings were worn in pairs.

9 Top: Finger ring with griffon motif, from the north female grave in kurgan 22 near Krasnyi Perekop. The ring is made of electrum, an alloy of gold and silver (Photo:Leskov).

10 Right: Armour and weapons of the king in the side grave of the Solocha kurgan; see fig. 47. Reconstruction based on the archaeological finds, by M.V. Gorelik.

11 Details from the frieze of figures on the amphora from the Čertomlyk kurgan; see p.104ff. Above: the front legs are hobbled before pasture.

12 Below: Training scene from the same frieze.

13 Above: Magnificent gold decorated comb from the side grave of the Solocha kurgan, showing Scythians in battle. End of the fifth/beginning of the fourth century BC. 4.8 in. (12.3 cm) high, 10.4 oz (294 g). For details see p. 74f.

**14** Gold pectoral 12 in. (30.6 cm) wide, weighing 3.3 lb (1.5 kg), from the central grave of the Tolstaya mogila of Ordžonikidze. Second half of the fourth century BC. For details of this breast ornament see also figs. 29 and 72–5.

**15** Above: Centre scene of the upper frieze: two Scythians making a shirt of animal skin, or mail armour (Photo: Kločko).

**16** Below: Young Scythian milking a sheep (Photo:Kločko).

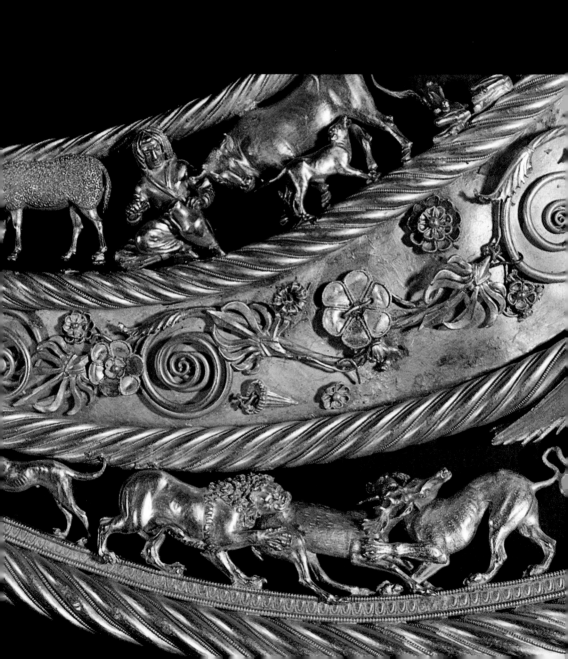

17  Detail from the pectoral, colour plate 14. Young Scythian sealing the amphora filled with milk (above). On the left the sheep which has been milked, on the right a cow with a suckling calf. Below: a lion and a cheetah tearing a stag to pieces.

19 Top left: Gold shield ornament: panther in typical Scythian animal-art style, from a Kelermes kurgan. Sixth century BC.

20 Bottom left: Gold shield ornament: stag lying down or hunting, from the Kul'-Oba kurgan. Fifth/fourth century BC.

21 Below: Gold 'curled-up animal' from Peter the Great's Siberian collection (function of ornament not known).

**22  Gold beaker from the Kul'-Oba kurgan
with scenes of warrior life. See fig. 40.**

and sometimes even over a thousand arrows serving as reserves for several quivers, which would be rendered razor-sharp before battle.

The typical Scythian bow is a small composite bow, i.e. assembled from a single wooden core whose ends were additionally reinforced with special coverings (string wrapped round and glued on, together with plates of bone). We can deduce from the evidence that there were also bows of over three feet (1 m) in length.

The Scythians seem to have been the inventors of a special combined bow-case and quiver, called the *gorytus*, which was worn hanging from the belt. While the men were stalking or before direct contact with the enemy, the stringed bow was kept in this case; a special pocket at the front for the arrows could be closed with a flap, probably to keep out moisture and protect the feathering. This combined case and quiver guaranteed the immediate readiness to shoot of 'professional' archers. In pictures, the Scythians are usually shown carrying two *goryti*, doubtless so that, together with the appropriate bow, the archer had the sizes and types of arrows necessary for any hunting and fighting situation immediately to hand. In order to render the wound even nastier and the removal of the arrow more difficult, thorns were fixed to the arrowheads.

We learn from written sources that the arrows were poisoned, and a recipe for Scythian arrow poison can be approximately reconstructed from information given by Theophrastus, Aristotle and Pliny. To produce it, the Scythians caught a certain kind of snake (probably small adders) at a fixed time of year, leaving their bodies to decompose. They then filled vessels with human blood, which they sealed and buried in dung until the blood began to putrefy. The decayed matter floating in the blood was mixed with the substances extracted from the decomposed adders to form a pernicious poison which in ancient times was called *scythicon* or *toxicon*.

The snake poison presumably retained its potency in the decomposed bodies of the adders, the blood was an excellent breeding-ground for bacteria, and the dung contained tetanus and gangrene germs. We can imagine the stages by which the poison took its course: if the arrow did not cause immediate death, the snake poison would probably take effect within an hour. There would be disintegration of the blood corpuscles, probably also shock effects and possibly respiratory paralysis. If the victim survived, gangrene would set in after about a day and possibly also suppuration of the wound. After an incubation period of one to two days, or perhaps not until a week later, tetanus would set in.[9]

'Some fall, pitifully shot down by hooked arrows; for a poisonous juice clings to the flying metal' is Ovid's poetic description of the use of the Scythian's main weapon; he refers to it as a missile 'which promises a double death'. These arrowheads, fitted with hooks and soaked in poison, were particularly feared, since they were very difficult to remove from the wound and caused the victim great pain during the process. Not only this, but the poison was calculated to cause long-term damage and even slight wounds were therefore likely to prove fatal.

Apart from snake poison, which they were also able to use for curative purposes, the Scythians used hemlock, which in some written sources is also numbered among their 'weapons'.

Their proficiency in archery – they were ambidextrous in the handling of the bow – and their way of living and fighting on horseback earned the Scythians the Greek term 'horse-archers'. They seem to have achieved a remarkable degree of accuracy, as is confirmed by a series of burial finds. Since the arrowheads were often not removed from the body but remained stuck in the bone, it has been possible to establish that an enemy had been struck by a shot right between the eyes from on horseback.

We have only an approximate idea of the range of the bow, since no original specimen has survived. An inscription from Olbia on the Black Sea extols the shooting range of the Olbian Anaxagoras, who in a festive competition won the prize for long-distance shooting with a distance of over 1640 ft (500 m). Here in the region north of the Black

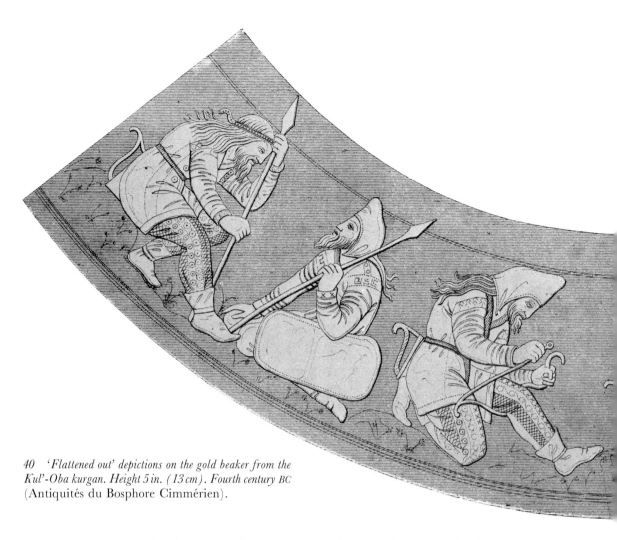

*40  'Flattened out' depictions on the gold beaker from the Kul'-Oba kurgan. Height 5 in. (13 cm). Fourth century BC (Antiquités du Bosphore Cimmérien).*

Sea, Anaxagoras probably used a Scythian bow, and the emergence of a new competition of this kind may also have been due to the influence of the indigenous population on the Greek colonials. The arrow would of course have the power to penetrate only at a much shorter distance. A Scythian battle probably began with a hail of arrows, similar to that of medieval horse-riding nomads. This thick 'cloud' of arrows could obscure the sun – a very plausible description – if we bear in mind that a practised archer, as we know from ethnological parallels, can shoot around twenty arrows a minute.

The method of stringing the bow differed from that of today; the knee was used as a support, as shown in ancient depictions such as the scene on the famous electrum vessel from the Kul'-Oba burial mound, which apparently portrays the phases before and after battle. The composite bow was of such elasticity that when slackened its 'arms' sprang back, forming an almost semicircular curve. For this reason such bows are described as reflex bows. We know from ethnological and historical evidence that a composite bow of this nature would have taken between five and ten years to produce, as special types of wood and horsehair string were used, and long periods of seasoning were necessary. In addition there would be a 'shooting-in' phase.

The arms of the Scythian warrior élite were cleverly adapted to suit all possible distances and situations in battle. After the bow and arrow the lance and spear were used, and in hand-to-hand fighting the axe (*sagaris*), the long and short sword, a kind of miniature chain flail, and a whip similar to that used by the Cossacks were brought into action.

It was not the great quantity of weapon

finds alone, however, which led to the decisive breakthrough towards a fundamentally different evaluation of Scythian warfare. Important new emphases, which must also be borne in mind when assessing fighting tactics and strength, have emerged primarily from the large-scale investigations of the Kiev archaeologist E.V. Cernenko. These mainly concerned armour, and were to change radically the reconstruction of the fully-armed Scythian warrior. The customary hackneyed view found in literature, that mounted nomad warriors were wandering hordes, who in favourable circumstances were prepared to attack but who on meeting firm resistance took flight as fast as possible no longer holds true. The idea of lightly-armed archers, whose main advantage lay in the swiftness of their horses and who avoided pitched battles, succeeding less through personal bravery than through clever tactics, has to be revised.

The very first studies of Cernenko showed that since the sixth century BC there was at least a core of heavily-armoured riders in a Scythian army, whose numbers increased in subsequent centuries. The manufacture of the various types of scale armour was particularly impressive. Such armour consisted of many thousands of bronze or iron scales attached to a leather jerkin, so that about a third of every scale was covered by the next. The size of the individual scales varied widely. We know of armour with very small, carefully polished scales of about 0.7 × 0.3 in. (1.7 × 0.7 cm) in size, and also of cruder types. The scales were all attached individually and layered one above the other, and quite often each metal scale was lined with one of leather. All this increased the flexibility and comfort of the armour, and presumably also made necessary

*41 Detail from the gold beaker from the Kul'-Oba kurgan, showing two armed Scythians after hunting or battle. The one on the left is injured, and the one on the right is applying a bandage.*

repairs easier. Scale armour had to be carefully looked after, if only to ensure that it did not rust. According to recent evidence it was lined inside with animal skin, or even made completely of skin, which probably lessened the friction and absorbed the sweat.

Besides coats of armour the Scythians also devised other forms of scale armour, from helmets to breeches for the protection of the thighs and knees. In addition, they wore heavy fighting belts trimmed with strips of iron which protected the loins. Their shields were often covered with iron plates and could be carried on the back so that the warriors remained protected and their hands could be kept free for battle. The most recent excavations have revealed several 'iron knights', skeletons covered almost from head to toe in iron scales, with their shields by their sides. They must originally have resembled armed Japanese *samurai*, producing the same sounds of clinking metal as they moved.

The preparations for an imminent military campaign must accordingly have involved much bustling activity: with hordes of warriors on excited, neighing steeds with pack-horses and large quantities of provisions; field tents or *yurts*, and carts in a colourful throng; armourers, bow-makers and leather-workers plying their trade for all they were worth, the clink of armour being cleaned and repaired, the whirr of bowstrings, and above all the sharpening of swords, lances and double axes as sharp as pick-axes. Many hundreds of arrows, their points needle-sharp, would be feathered and (perhaps amid murmurings of magic formulae) poisoned, and incendiary arrows prepared. Then a signal would announce the appearance of the King, and after a magnificent parade the army would noisily set off.

We have no precise idea as to the magic rituals which preceded Scythian campaigns. We know from information about later horse-riding nomadic peoples how complicated and imbued with superstitious notions such

42 *High-ranking Scythians in full armour. On the right is the prince from the Tolstaya mogila of Ordžonikidze. Reconstructions based on modern archaeological finds by M.V. Gorelik.*

campaigns were. For the Scythian soothsayers, who according to Herodotus prophesied from willow rods, business must have been booming.

As we might expect, even the 'sceptres' of the kings and other leaders of the Scythian fighting units took the form of weapons. The flail sceptres found indicate a scale of degree based on the metal used. Three finds of such sceptres have been discovered to date; these are made of lead and bronze, and it is possible that in future excavations Scythian leaders will be discovered with silver and gold sceptres.

From the large quantity of costly weapons found, which were possibly status symbols and marks of honour, we can reconstruct the weapons and armour, bristling with gold, of the mounted Scythian warrior. Even at its most opulent, such weaponry always had some practical use. According to all the written sources the Scythian kings invariably took an active part in battle at the head of their army.

The same applied generally to the Scythian nobility, whose burial deposits show them to have been heavily-armed cavalry warriors and whose skeletons often show traces of wounds.

## The 'Scythian route'

Most Scythian weapons of attack were designed to break down the resistance of armed warriors, but the effectiveness of their own protective armour throws an interesting light on the attacking power of their enemies, especially in the Near East and Asia Minor, where the Scythians launched extensive campaigns from the seventh century BC at the latest.

As early as the eighth century BC there is mention of marauding hordes invading the Near East from the north via the Caucasus, in ancient Eastern and later in Greek written sources. *Gimmirri* and *ashkuzai* are the names most frequently used to refer to them. As a scourge of apocalyptic proportions they are even mentioned in the Bible:

'Lo, I will bring a nation upon you from far, O house of Israel...it is a mighty nation, it is an ancient nation, a nation whose language thou knowest not, neither understandest what they say. Their quiver is as an open sepulchre, they are all mighty men.

And they shall eat up thine harvest, and thy bread, which thy sons and thy daughters should eat: they shall eat up thy flocks and thine herds: they shall eat up thy vines and thy fig trees: they shall impoverish thy fenced cities, wherein thou trustest, with the sword.' (Jeremiah, 5: 15–17)

'Behold, a people shall come from the north, and a great nation, and many kings shall be raised up from the coasts of the earth. They shall hold the bow and the lance: they are cruel, and will not shew mercy: their voice shall roar like the sea, and they shall ride upon horses, every one put in array, like a man to battle, against thee, O daughter of Babylon.' (Jeremiah, 50: 41–2)

These peoples are taken by many scholars to be the Cimmerians and Scythians, and numerous archaeological finds indicate that they were indeed present in the ancient Orient.

The complicated history of these large-scale campaigns – perhaps, in part, attempts to acquire land which continued for several

*43  Invasion routes into the Near East. Cartographic representation by Krupnov.*

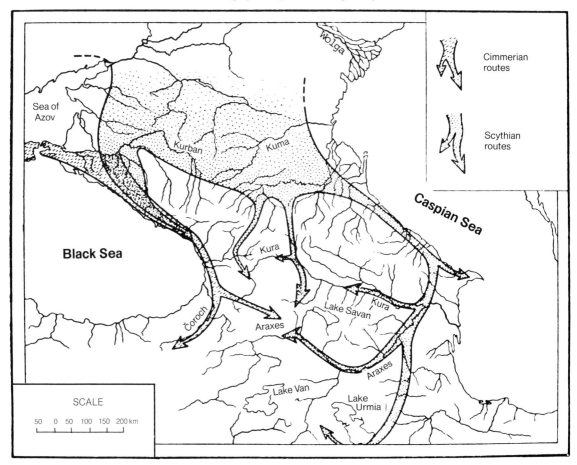

centuries – would fill a separate volume and can only be touched on here.

In overcoming the geographical difficulties alone, the military expedition of the mounted nomad forces into the Near East represented a remarkable achievement. For the way to all the riches and beauties of the Near East was blocked by the steep mountains of the Caucasus ('Duris cautibus, horrens Caucasus!', Virgil), which, owing to its impassable terrain, has from ancient times formed a barrier separating nations and peoples.

'There is a route which leads from the nomads in the north to Iberia. It involves an arduous three-day climb followed by a descent along a gorge formed by the river Argos, where men and animals have to walk in single file' writes Strabo, adding that it was estimated to have taken four days, showing that the central Kreuzberg Pass was in use by the first millennium BC at the latest.

The Kreuzberg Pass, also called the 'Caucasus Gate', is the only pass which for much of the year is free from ice and traversable. The Caucasus passes lie at even greater altitudes than those of the Alps. If we consider the difficulties involved in crossing the Alps in ancient times – as in the case of Hannibal for example – we have an approximate idea of the organization and powers of endurance of the Scythian forces, first penetrating into the south and later streaming back north. Their ability to negotiate this difficult north-south route led to the term 'Scythian route' being applied to the Caucasus.

If it is correct to equate the *ashkuzai* (*Iškuza*) with the Scythians (and there is much to support this theory), one of the first Scythians known to us by name is a king, Partatua, who sent a messenger to the Assyrian King Asarhaddon asking for the hand of one of the latter's daughters in marriage. The Assyrian King, unsure whether the suitor would keep his word and greatly fearing his military powers, turned to the god Šamaš with an oracular question, as was the custom at the time. He wanted to know whether his future son-in-law would indeed do 'everything' which would benefit him, Asarhaddon. The god's answer was ascertained by the Assyrians through the examination of animals' entrails. This involved the opening up of an animal (usually a sheep) and the close scrutiny of the various features of its innards: how the intestines lay, what the kidneys were like (a missing kidney augured ill, a small kidney was important); the nature of the liver was crucial. Any peculiarity, for example an unusual colouring, defects, disorders, hypertrophies, was interpreted, even the relationship of the parts to each other.

We do not know exactly how the story of the marriage between the Scythian King and the Assyrian Princess turned out – whether the gall bladder of the sacrificial sheep was in the correct position or its intestines jerked at the right moment... but we can assume that the Scythian did indeed receive his Assyrian lady in marriage, since he is mentioned as an ally of the Assyrian King. The latter may perhaps not have been overjoyed at his daughter's *mésalliance*, but it was nevertheless useful to have such a son-in-law. In those days too, princesses would hardly have been asked whom they wanted to marry, although for a lady accustomed to a life of luxury in an Assyrian palace, life as companion to a barbarian king cannot always have been easy.

Against the background of these close dynastic interconnections between Assyrians and Scythians, certain historical events and pieces of archaeological evidence relating to these relationships begin to make sense. Herodotus informs us, for instance, that Madyas – apparently a son of King Partatua – advanced with a large Scythian army to relieve the besieged Assyrian capital of Nineveh and annihilated the Medes. If we accept the idea that Assurbanipal (669–626 BC) may have been his uncle, we can understand why he was so committed.

Herodotus gives a retrospective description of these campaigns long past (I, 103ff.; IV, 1, 11–12), which in his account appear as one great military operation. According to him the Scythians originally came from the east, penetrating the area north of the Black Sea as immigrants, where they encountered the indigenous Cimmerians. The latter, fearful of the approaching danger and divided as to the

best defence strategy, killed their kings who were determined to do battle and fled before the Scythians along the Black Sea and into the Near East. Their pursuit of the Cimmerians also took the Scythians into the Near East, where they passed the Caucasus mountains to their right; we can thus assume that they advanced along the Caspian Sea by the route leading through Derbent. After the relief of Nineveh and their victory over the Medes, the Scythians, according to Herodotus, had controlled the whole of the Near East for 28 years, causing havoc and confusion, not to mention the tribute they forcibly extracted. But then, continues Herodotus, the Median

King Cyaxares managed to make a large number of them drunk and then murder them. The survivors returned to the north Pontic steppes, where they had to do battle with the sons of the wives they had left behind – these sons being the fruit of the women's union with slaves during the protracted absence of their husbands. The strong resistance could only be broken, according to the legend, by means of 'psychological warfare': forced into a choice between falling in battle, thus decimating their own numbers, or killing off many of their own slaves and leaving themselves in short supply, the Scythians are said to have adopted the tactic of striding towards the

44 Top: Depiction of a battle between Greeks and mounted warriors on a sarcophagus from Klazomenai (Murray).

45 Left: Mounted backward-shooting archers with pointed caps on a Greek vase (Minns).

46 Right: Depiction of mounted Scythian troops on a black-figure water jar in the Vatican Museum (Schauenburg).

rebellious slaves with whips, thus reminding them of their inferior state and pointing out to them the uselessness of further revolt.

Historically and archaeologically the whip has been in evidence right up until recent times in the region north of the Black Sea, as both weapon and status symbol. Ancient portrayals of noble Scythians show the latter in relaxed attitude, with a Cossack-type whip (*nagaica*)[10] in their raised hands. This consisted of a short, firm handle bound in gold tape, and leather thongs which were probably knotted. Wielded skilfully this was an accurate and terrible weapon, especially when used against the unprotected face of the enemy. Just how successful such whips were against even heavily-armoured knights is shown in an episode from the journal of the 'Master of Ceremonies of the Great Gate' during the Turkish siege of Vienna. According to this account, a heavily-armoured 'infidel' was brought before Kara Mustapha, the Turkish commander-in-chief, on 23 July 1683. He had been taken prisoner near Linz by the Crimean Tatar allies who were 'swift as the wind'. The war journal states that he had boasted that no musket-ball could penetrate his armour, and when this was put to the test it proved to be true. On being asked by the Turks how he was nevertheless taken prisoner by the Tatars, especially as he had had the advantage of horse and lance, he replied: 'They beat me about the face and eyes with their whips until they could unseat me and tie me up.'[11]

The Cossacks still used this weapon in the nineteenth century: 'But a real steppe Cossack needs neither musket nor bracket [to hunt wolves] but only his well-plaited *nagaica* (*kanchu*). He pursues the wolf with it, and after riding alongside it for a while he cuts it down with this wonder-weapon of his.'[12] A Tatar or Cossack could split an enemy's skull with the *nagaica*, and the Kirghizians used it to kill leopards.

As long as they still held the *nagaica* in their hands the inhabitants of the north Pontic steppes refused to give in, writes Kohl in the first half of the nineteenth century. He goes on: 'When these peoples have shot their arrows and bullets and broken their lances, and

engage in hand-to-hand fighting, it is the *nagaicas* that are decisive. It is not action with pistol or sabre that determines the victor, but whip combat.'

## 'They call that heroism . . .'[13]

What the end of a battle was like in Scythian times is conveyed by a small work of art from the fourth century BC: the famous golden comb from the Solocha kurgan (colour plate 13).

In 1913 the Russian archaeologist N.I. Veselovski succeeded in uncovering a royal Scythian tomb which had not been looted by grave-robbers. The Solocha kurgan and its riches was reported throughout the world's press. This ruler's burial equipment, even today, is still the most impressive known to us from the world of horse-riding nomads. The weapons are magnificently worked in silver and gold, as are the numerous eating and drinking vessels which were given to the dead for use in the next world. Many and various are the portrayals of hunting and fighting scenes decorating the weapons and bowls.

Of special significance is a golden comb weighing 10.4 oz (294 g) and 4.9 in. (12.3 cm) high, with long, four-sided teeth. Its handle depicts a very dramatic and precisely portrayed battle scene involving three Scythians: a rider in the centre, with his adversary before him (on the right) who can only continue battle on foot – standing between the back legs of his badly wounded and fallen horse – and a third warrior rushing in from the left, presumably to help the rider in the middle. This heavily-armoured rider, wearing helmet, scale armour, plated shield and greaves, has apparently injured his enemy's horse with a short spear; it lies bleeding from two wounds – behind the left shoulder and on the right-hand side of the chest – and it seems from the position of the legs that it is not dead but jerking on the ground. In spite of his armour he shows himself to be an excellent rider: holding the reins in his left hand he is pulling his horse round to the left on its hindquarters, so that it almost has to step on the head of

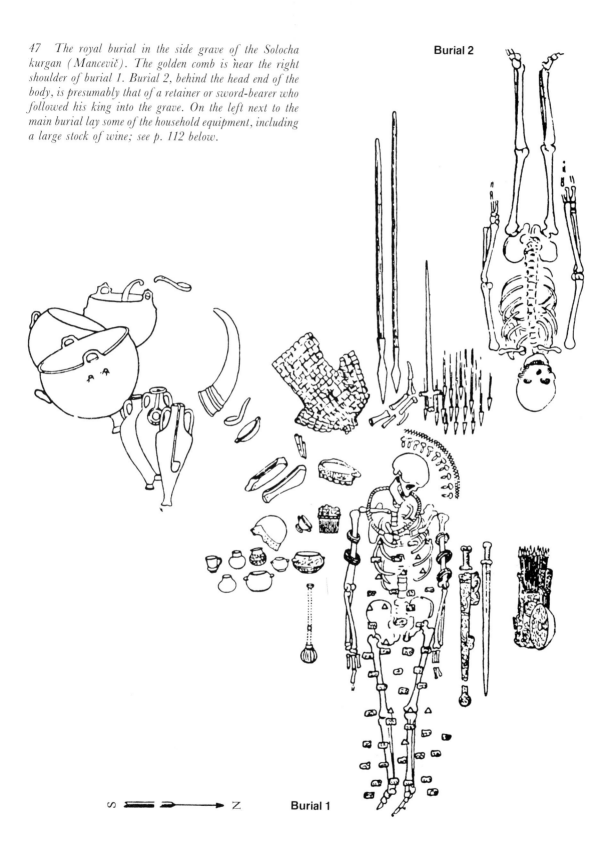

**Burial 2**

47 The royal burial in the side grave of the Solocha kurgan (Mancevič). The golden comb is near the right shoulder of burial 1. Burial 2, behind the head end of the body, is presumably that of a retainer or sword-bearer who followed his king into the grave. On the left next to the main burial lay some of the household equipment, including a large stock of wine; see p. 112 below.

S ⟸⟹ ⟶ N   **Burial 1**

75

48 *The Solocha kurgan during the excavations in 1912/13. A looted central grave and an intact side grave were discovered inside.*

49 *Cross-section of the side grave in the mound, whose shaft descended 17.8 ft (5.40 m) below the original surface and was connected to the burial chamber by a passage 36 ft (11 m) long (Veselovski).*

50 *Top right: Gold-plated silver bowl from the side grave of the Solocha kurgan showing Scythians hunting fabulous creatures.*

51 *Bottom right: Detail of the reverse side of the above.*

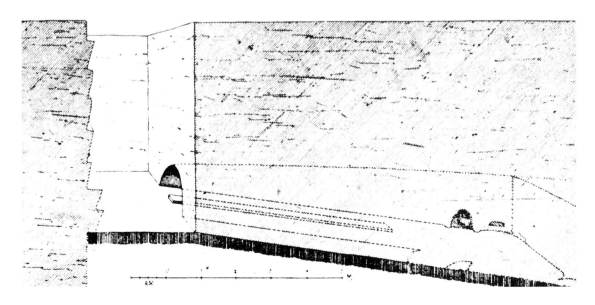

52,53 *Facial expressions of the two adversaries on the Solocha comb (see colour plate 13). On the left is the rider in the centre, on the right his opponent fighting on foot (Mancevič).*

the injured horse lying on the ground. Raising itself on its forelegs it just manages to avoid the jerking forelegs of the fallen horse. The laid-back ears, wide open rolling eyes and flaring nostrils reflect the drama of the scene. Positively trembling, but with all the indications of absolute obedience and trust in its rider, this animal portrays the type of Scythian horse which owing to battle training could merge with its rider into a single fighting unit.

The rider is trying to take advantage of his horse's turning movement to hurl his lance at his enemy and break his shield. He scorns the protection afforded by his iron-plated shield, wearing it on his back so that his hands remain free for battle. From his expression of calm confidence it seems that the fatal blow – he is doubtless aiming at his enemy's unprotected throat area – is about to strike home. Just how menacing and unassailable the oncoming rider and his steed seem from the perspective his enemy – on the left – is shown in fig. 54.

The latter must also be aware of the silhouette of a second adversary looming in the background.

This is the depiction of the final phase of a battle scene. Not only is the particular stage of the engagement shown, but also the fact that the warriors no longer have all their weapons. Thus only the empty bow-case and quiver is still hanging at the rider's hip. The arrows will have been used up from a distance and the bow destroyed or perhaps lost in the fray. The only weapon still available to him is the apparently broken spear. His adversary is defending himself with a short dagger, which is obviously not meant for the long sword-sheath at his left side: his sword has presumably been lost in battle like his other weapons. The warrior rushing in from the left only has an empty quiver at his side. If he had a protective helmet it too has gone astray.

The facial expressions of the three warriors are all quite different. The rider's face expresses

*54   The advancing rider from the perspective of his adversary. His armour and rearing horse make it impossible to get close to him. In the background the silhouette of another enemy can be discerned.*

a calm assurance of victory and an awareness of his own superiority of weapon, while the warrior standing over his fallen horse shows an iron determination not to give in. The soldier rushing in on foot is completely mesmerized by the scene confronting him.

It is interesting to note that both horses are without saddles. Considering the otherwise heavily armoured riders, this is probably a motif used to highlight the unusual nature of the scene: riding without a saddle was normally portrayed only in hunting scenes.

The artist has captured the end of an engagement as in a snapshot. The drama of the scene and its conclusion would doubtless have been obvious to anybody who had himself been involved in such a battle situation. He would have been able to appreciate the rider's difficulties and the intensity of the fight, and to predict accurately a victory over the warrior on foot, who was doubtless the rider's equal in rank.

The central and most outstanding feature of the representation is the face of the rider (as opposed to that of his adversary), which can be seen equally well from both sides. In fact it is clear from the precision of the workmanship that each side of the comb was meant to be visible.

This magnificent comb lay in the grave beside the right shoulder of the dead man. Its function as a comb seems at first obvious, but the fact that the scene depicted on it would have been hidden by the hand in the action of combing indicates rather that it was used decoratively. This presupposes a headdress on to which the comb could be fixed. It is however quite possible that on certain occasions the king wore it in his long hair which may have been tied up in a knot. There is an ancient depiction of two warriors with such a hairstyle, similar to the modern pony-tail. The comb, fixed to this kind of hairstyle, would have been clearly visible from both sides – a kind

55 *Top left: Silver, in part gold-plated bow-case and quiver from the Solocha kurgan, depicting Scythians in battle (Stepanov).*

56 *Bottom left: Battle between Greeks and native barbarians. Scene on a gold Akinakes scabbard from kurgan 8 of the 'five-brother' group near Elisavetinskaya Stanica in the Don district (Photo: Silov).*

57 *Top: Scythians fighting back to back, surrounded by the enemy (blood brothers?) (Or des Scythes).*

58 *Right: Mounted warrior returning home after battle. Bow and arrows and the whip in the right hand, are recognizable, as is the severed head of an enemy hanging from the reins. Motif on a belt from the cemetery of Tli, Caucasus (Techov).*

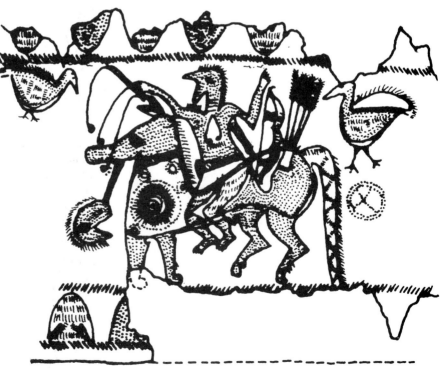

of 'crown', which was presumably the actual function of this work of art. The Scythians were a people for whom courage and fighting ability were the highest ideals and whose kings actually did fulfil the role of military leaders. The test of courage depicted on the comb would have corresponded exactly to their ideas of personal bravery and valour in battle which marked out a Scythian ruler and distinguished him in the eyes of his warriors.

Today it is no longer possible to establish whether the portrayal on the comb shows an episode from the life of the buried king or one of his ancestors. There is some likelihood that the former is the case, especially as a similar helmet, though somewhat modified in form, was found with the body.

The emphasis in the Scythian world was on fighting, and they led spartan lives constantly threatened by danger and injury. The smell of blood and corpses was common, and they killed to protect their possessions and to avoid being killed themselves. Blood accordingly ranked high in the Scythian order of things: symbolically, when on the battlefield a warrior would drink the blood of the first man he killed, or practically, when in an emergency he would bleed his horse in order to survive with the help of its blood.

The amount of a warrior's loot was often related in antiquity to the number of enemy heads he had collected. This custom is depicted on life-size reliefs throughout the Near East, in which severed heads heaped up before the victors are being meticulously recorded. (Such headhunting was of course practised far beyond this region – for instance in Central Europe among Celts and Germanic tribes – but we do not have such vivid representations in this case and are therefore dependent on written sources and archaeological finds.)

Various authors of antiquity report that the Scythians also collected the severed heads of their enemies and brought them before the king. It was not only the loot that was apportioned according to the number of heads, but also the degree of honour bestowed on a warrior at the annual 'stocktaking'. At this ceremony a large vessel was filled with wine, and poured out by the governor of the district (the *nomarch*) for the warriors who had been successful in battle. To have to sit to one side in ignominy – having killed no enemies – was considered by the Scythians to be the worse disgrace possible (Herodotus IV, 66). A cylindrical gold plate, the top of a headdress which itself no longer survives, appears to depict in primitive form a handing over of heads to the prince or king.

We also learn that the Scythians used the tops of their enemies' skulls as drinking bowls. These were covered in leather, and also gilded on the inside by the rich. The insult to the dead implied in this custom probably went hand in hand with the idea that the power of the enemy could be absorbed in this way. It was the Scythian practice to skin the enemy's corpse, especially the scalp. The skin was then tanned, and the warriors would show it off (writes Herodotus) by using it as a towel or in the case of the scalps as decorative handkerchiefs tied to their horses' bridles.

In antiquity scalping was considered so typically Scythian that the Greeks invented a special verb to denote the process. The term *aposkythizein* was applied to skinning the head, and we are also told that to lose the hair from one's head was considered a disgrace.

59  *Depiction of the handing over of a head, on a gold-ornamented cap from a kurgan near Kurdžips (Minns).*

'They consider tattooing a mark of high birth, the lack of it a mark of low birth.' (Herodotus, V, 6, of the Thracians). We have known at least since the discovery of a magnificently tattooed mummy in one of the Pazyryk kurgans (kurgan 2) that ancient reports of this kind of decoration in the region north of the Black Sea were not unfounded. The body of this man was decorated all over with ornate animal-style motifs, only some of which have been well preserved. The composition is not arbitrary: the arrangement of the animal figures reveals an important language of symbols – the whole is presumably an individual pictorial programme of 'dynamic body-art'. The man from kurgan 2 must have been a walking work of art with 'living' motifs, since the animals would have appeared to move as the muscles were flexed. After being tattooed the man had filled out considerably – and with him some of the animal pictures which had been engraved and then rubbed into the skin with soot. Such tattoos may have provided a particular incentive to flay a dead enemy, i.e. skin him, tan the skin and make garments from it.

Although our precise knowledge of these phenomena stems from written sources alone, archaeological excavations, meanwhile, have also contributed with a series of finds. The most recent excavations on the *gorodišče* of Bel'sk (see p.117ff.) have uncovered a skull-cup 'workshop' with several human skull-tops which had already been made into drinking bowls with handles made from temple bones. There is archaeological evidence of the practice of scalping in some skull finds showing traces of the relevant incisions. The most impressive observations, however, were made on the tattooed warrior from the second kurgan mentioned above. After an examination of the body it was possible to reconstruct one of the dramatic battle engagements of the time. The man was already between 50 and 60 at his death. Three battle-axe wounds, all inflicted from different directions and apparently from behind, indicate that he had been caught in an ambush, killed and scalped. After this his own people must somehow have managed to recover the body. In the

*60   Details of the body-tattooing in fig. 61.*

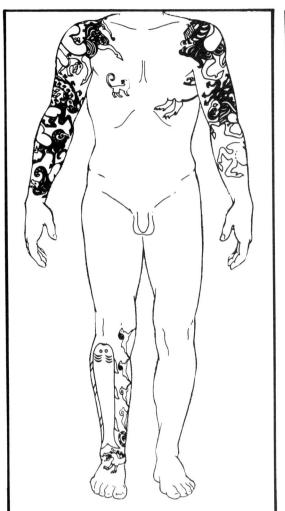

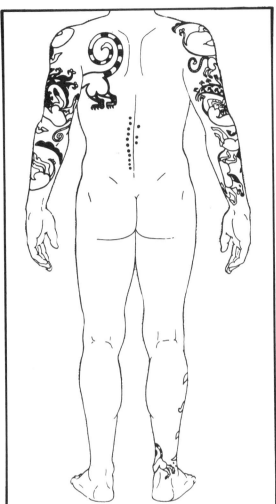

84

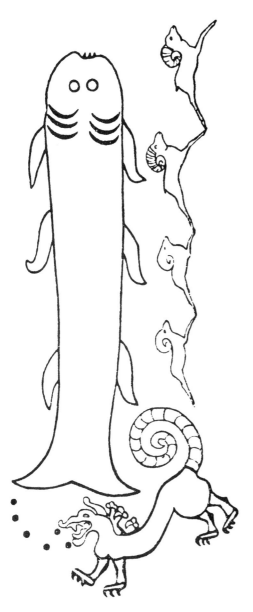

Scythians' idea of the next world, the absence of head-hair signified a great lack, and the loss was therefore concealed by a scalp sewn with horsehair. Since there has as yet been no detailed forensic examination, we do not know whether this practical device involved the sewing on of the man's own (recovered) scalp, or a substitute scalp procured from an enemy, or even an 'artificial scalp' resembling a wig.

A further example of the way the steppe people fought is seen in the skeleton of a fatally wounded (early Sarmatian) warrior, found in Krasnogorsk (near Orsk). The victors had beheaded him, presumably taking the head with them as a trophy – at any rate there was no skull in the grave. The lower legs were separated from the body and had no doubt been hacked off. There were six arrowheads embedded in the skeleton and their positions showed in part the direction from which they had come. The first was below the right shoulder-blade and the second at the back of the left shoulder-blade. The third was under the shoulder, the fourth in the wrist, the fifth in the heart area and the sixth in the left knee.

A coat decorated at the neck with gold and a sword also lavishly covered in gold indicate that this was a rich warrior who had died in a hail of enemy arrows and then been butchered. His head probably gained honour

*61   Tattooing on the male body from the 2nd Pazyryk kurgan. General view front and back, and details (Rudenko and Artamonov).*

and a good share of loot for the victor.

The fact that victory *alone* was the goal to which the Scythians' every action was geared, becomes evident in our final survey of the notorious failure of the Persian campaign of 513 BC, described above (p.7). The campaign was launched against the European Scythians under their king, Idanthyrsus. The Persian forces were so impressive that failure seemed absolutely inconceivable. After the resounding defeat of their army in 529 under Darius's predecessor Cyrus the Great, (whose head ended up as a trophy in the hands of the Queen of the Massagetae, Tomyris), Darius himself attempted to pacify the northern flank of his empire. He was at first victorious over the Asian Scythians and their King, Skuka, whose successor he chose. Then began the campaign against the European Scythians, who drove Darius to despair with their trick of tactical retreat – supposed to have been a Scythian invention. An analysis of Darius's campaign as described by Herodotus (Book IV) shows that the Scythian action was characterized by flexibility and a precise estimation of the enemy's strength. Furthermore, by skilful, cunning evasive action they could force the place and time of battle on their enemy. Not obsessed with fighting 'chivalrously', yet reacting with extreme sensitivity to any slur on their honour, the Scythians were motivated by their code of behaviour to a high degree of personal courage and self-sacrifice – if it was a question of something which closely concerned them.

## The 'man-killers' – female all-round athletes of antiquity

Numerous myths and legends grew up around women or bands of women in ancient times, who fought either alongside men or alone against them. The Greeks called such women Amazons, and we have the Scythian word for them from the region north of the Black Sea: *Oiorpata*. Herodotus informs us (IV, 110) that this term derived from the words *oior* (man) and *pata* (to kill).

Probably the best known female 'troop' of antiquity was the army from the south coast of the Black Sea, at whose head Penthesilea, Queen of the Amazons (and according to legend a daughter of Ares) entered Troy after the death of Hector. The Penthesilea myth appears in various legends at different times, undergoing considerable changes in motif. The most detailed source on the subject is Quintus of Smyrna, who tells in his poetry of the beautiful Penthesilea, fully armed and leading her comrades into battle amidst great jubilation. He does not, however, omit to express his disapproval of such unseemly female behaviour. The armour of the young female mounted warrior consisted of helmet, breastplate, greaves and *pelta* (shield in the shape of a double half-moon). Her weapons were sword, double-edged axe and two spears; she also used bow and arrows, her swift horse carrying the quiver. After initial success in battle Penthesilea's comrades perish, she herself continuing to decimate the ranks of the Greeks with battle-axe and spear until finally Ajax and Achilles appear on the battlefield. Her two throws with the spear are too weak to pose a serious threat to the two Greeks, and her fate is sealed. Derided by Achilles and impaled on her steed by a violent thrust of the spear, she perishes with her horse.

The watching Trojan women, eager to join in the fighting, had been reminded of their lack of military training and sent back to their needlework. It was only the Amazons, they were told, who enjoyed the otherwise male activity of riding, and whose limbs and courage had been strengthened by constant warfare.

Greek women were excluded from contests generally, and even princesses like Cyniska and Belistiche, who were named in the list of victors, were in reality merely the owners of the teams of horses, not their drivers. Cyniska was nevertheless the first recorded female horse breeder of antiquity, and there must have been parallels in Scythia, especially as the women's area of responsibility there involved horse rearing even more than it did in Greece. The women probably had a considerable quota of work to fulfil which demanded physical exertion on horseback. They were also entrusted with the safety of the herds and protection of the pasturelands when the menfolk were at war, wounded or dead. It is therefore not surprising to find descriptions of women who could defend themselves from attack, and of professional female warriors. Such accounts have long been relegated to the realm of legend, and indeed descriptions by ancient authors of the (to them) alien and shocking appearance of these warrior women, written sometimes with relish and sometimes in horror, or with a strong tinge of moral disapproval, often seem difficult to believe. Archaeological and anthropological studies of finds in the north Pontic and forest steppes have, however, since shown that these stories had a solid historical foundation.

In Book IV of Herodotus we find several Amazon stories from Scythia and Sauromatia (the Volga region), a country on Scythia's eastern border. The author tells in loving detail of an Amazon 'invasion' of a Scythian coast. He describes how shiploads of Amazon prisoners of war from Asia Minor overcame their Greek guards in the Black Sea and eventually found themselves in Lake Maeotis (the modern Sea of Asov). There the women seized horses and embarked upon a life of plunder, which soon led to a confrontation with the Scythians. During the battle, the Scythians discovered from the bodies which came into their possession that they were women. They were so impressed that they wanted children from these women, and they decided to avoid further battles and instead to approach them with guile. Young (and presumably attractive) warriors were sent to win the Amazons; they were to pitch camp near them and live a life of plunder and hunting just like them. Eventually the camps drew nearer, and one day, around midday, when the Amazons had spread out in order to relieve themselves, one of the youths succeeded in taking advantage of the situation with one of the women. The two were only able to communicate through signs and gestures, but they managed to arrange another meeting for the next day, when each would bring a partner with them. Within a short time the two camps were united. Eventually

the Amazons learnt the Scythian language and persuaded their men to demand their inheritance and journey with them for a few days eastwards, not least because they were convinced that they could not live together with the Scythian women:

'We are riders; our business is with the bow and the spear, and we know nothing of women's work. But in your country no woman has anything to do with such things – your women stay at home in their waggons occupied with feminine tasks, and never go out to hunt or for any other purpose.' (Herodotus IV, 114).

These *émigrés* became, according to legend, the founders of the Sauromatian tribe, and as the Amazons were never able to master the Scythian language adequately, the language of the Sauromatians was said to be a corrupt version of Scythian.

'Ever since then the women of the Sauromatae have kept to their old ways, riding to the hunt on horseback sometimes with, sometimes without, their menfolk, taking part in war and wearing the same sort of clothes as men.' (Herodotus IV, 116)

'They have a marriage law which forbids a girl to marry until she has killed an enemy in battle; some of their women, unable to fulfil this condition, grow old and die in spinsterhood.' (Herodotus IV, 117)

Several women's graves, whose inventories of grave goods include weapons, were unearthed as early as the last century during the excavations of Count A.A. Bobrinskoi near Smela. This excavator was one of the first to apply anthropological classification, and he soon recognized that these must be Amazon graves. Influenced by Herodotus's account, however, and on the basis of an erroneous dating of finds, he believed that the women he had discovered were Sauromatian. This error has now been corrected, and as numerous similar graves have been discovered during large-scale excavations in the southern Ukraine since the 1950s, it is now accepted that Amazon graves are to be found throughout the steppe region and probably even in the Caucasus.

We shall describe their typical features with the help of two particularly clear examples. The oldest known Amazon find is the centre burial in mound No. 20 on the Cholodny Yar on the left bank of the Tyasmin. It was discovered in a large, round burial ditch 14 ft (4.26 m) in diameter, under the remains of a timber ceiling. On the centre base of the ditch lay two skeletons. According to the anthropological classification, the first was female and lay supine pointing east/west. At its feet and lying on its right side lay a (probably) male skeleton of about 18 years of age. The relatively rich grave goods are almost without exception grouped around the main skeleton. The dead woman wore two large silver ear-rings, a necklace of bone and glass beads, and a bronze armring on her left arm. She had with her a bronze mirror, pottery, a clay spindle and food offerings together with the usual iron knives. At her head to the left lay two iron lance points, 22 in. (56 cm) and 18.9 in. (48 cm) long, with a smooth rectangular hone underneath them. On the left side of the skeleton lay the remains of a brightly painted quiver of wood and leather with 47 bronze treble-feathered arrowheads and two iron knives. Five 'pebble missiles' were also found near the skull. Next to the other skeleton, at the feet of the first, only two small bronze bells, two ornamental pipes and an iron armring were found. The grave dates from the fourth century BC.

A burial in kurgan 16 of Akkermen' I, in the Rayon Vasilevka, showed that women also wore armour. In one catacomb grave, just 9.8 ft (3 m) below the original surface and untouched by grave-robbers, lay the supine skeleton of a young woman. Among the grave goods were an armring, pearl necklaces and bracelets, a bronze mirror, a decorated spindle and the usual food offerings. In addition, the following weapons were found: a quiver containing 20 arrows, two lances lying to the left of the woman, and two further lances plunged into the ground beside each other at the grave entrance. There was also a heavy fighting belt covered in strips of iron. The

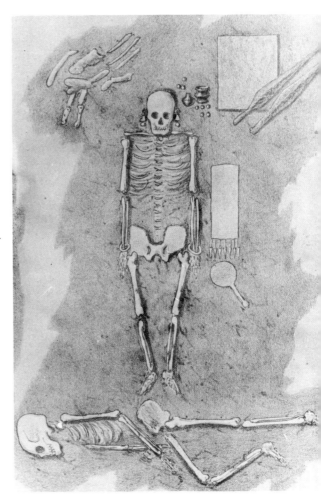

arrows were about 15.7 in. (40 cm) long and their ends were marked with painted red stripes 1.8 in. (4.5 cm) wide.

This grave reinforced for archaeologists the vital importance of detailed anthropological classification. In the past, graves containing weapons, and especially heavy armour, had with few exceptions been assumed to be those of men.

One might perhaps at first presume that these weapons were placed in women's graves – for some ritual reason unknown to us – without having been used by these women for hunting or in battle. But clear evidence of wounds – severe head injuries from blows and stabs, and a bent bronze arrowhead still embedded in the knee – contradicts this idea.

Written sources stress the connection of the Amazons of the region north of the Black Sea with Sauromatia, the lower Volga region, where the number of graves of armed women is indeed higher than in the Scythian region. Statistically, 20 per cent of graves containing weapons and harness in the Sauromatian area are those of women. This is a considerable proportion, and explains the interest shown in Sauromatia by the authors of antiquity. By far the most common weapon in the female graves here is the bow and arrow. In Scythia, however, on the western border, where over 40 such graves have so far been discovered, there is a group of *oiorpata* who had not only bows and arrows buried with them but combinations of various weapons: lances and spears, swords, daggers and pebbles (possibly for slings), also the metal-plated belts mentioned above for the protection of the loins. This relatively large and varied arsenal of weapons indicates a mastery of the different

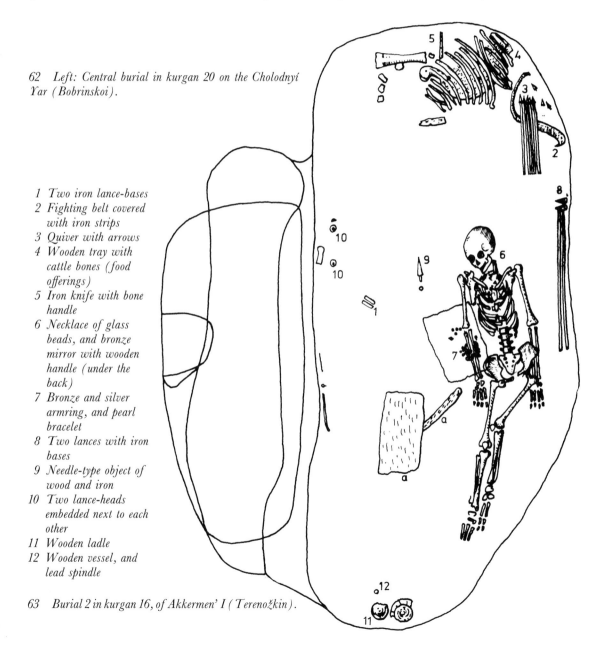

62    Left: Central burial in kurgan 20 on the Cholodnyí Yar (Bobrinskoi).

1  *Two iron lance-bases*
2  *Fighting belt covered with iron strips*
3  *Quiver with arrows*
4  *Wooden tray with cattle bones (food offerings)*
5  *Iron knife with bone handle*
6  *Necklace of glass beads, and bronze mirror with wooden handle (under the back)*
7  *Bronze and silver armring, and pearl bracelet*
8  *Two lances with iron bases*
9  *Needle-type object of wood and iron*
10 *Two lance-heads embedded next to each other*
11 *Wooden ladle*
12 *Wooden vessel, and lead spindle*

63    Burial 2 in kurgan 16, of Akkermen' I (Terenožkin).

martial skills.

Riding, so necessary for hunting and fighting, must have been learnt and practised from early youth onwards. In addition, there would be all-round training: overcoming obstacles, changing horses at a gallop, throwing and shooting at both fixed and moving targets, reckless games and the like. Long-distance riding would have been a major part of this training owing to the nomadic way of life in the north Pontic and Caspian steppe region and the great distances involved. Extensive training in the use of various weapons was doubtless also a requirement from childhood onwards.

Technical proficiency and expertise in the handling of their weapons must have been of supreme importance to the Amazons, whose physical strength was of course inferior to that of men. It is presumably no coincidence that the bow and arrow was their main weapon, being found in all Amazon graves. The bow and arrow compensated best for the weaker muscle power of the women, which remained inferior even when they had experienced intensive muscle training through various sports and hunting activities. As far as women are concerned the possibilities of lance, spear and javelin are limited from the outset, as the usually unfavourable angle of the arm bones allows a less effective transmission of strength than is the case with men. Of vital importance to the Amazons were stamina, strength, swiftness, skill and agility, all of which had to be acquired, as with the men, through specific and constant training. It is therefore not surprising to find weapons even in the graves of young girls. Hunting and fighting required an ability to react swiftly, and the bow as primary weapon demanded a calm concentration which was not easily diverted. Battles were fought on horseback and without stirrups, so absolute control of the animal in all situations was necessary, together with good co-ordination of eye, arm and breathing. An accurate sense of distance and excellent timing were also of paramount importance.

Because their physical training was so varied, the physique of these fighting women would in no way have resembled that of the 'mannish' women sometimes produced nowadays by intensive training for one particular competitive sport. We should presumably imagine them as being muscular but not heavy, as stamina and agility are adversely affected by weight. Their diet of mainly meat and their physical dexterity would probably ensure that they resembled rather the present-day type of all-round athlete and long-distance rider.

64 Depiction of an Amazon on a red-figure perfume casket in Odessa Museum (Sokolov); she is evidently examining the arrow for flaws.

These 'man-killers' were, however, for all that no less aware of their femininity and wished to retain their charms in the land of the dead, as the objects buried with them prove. They all have jewellery and mirrors, decorated according to the women's individual social rank; those interested in cosmetics also have make-up of various colours, and also scent bottles. Spindles were placed in the graves with them, presumably to make

clear that they could also do 'women's work'. We shall leave open the question of whether Amazon mothers, as stated by some ancient authors, really did burn off the right breast of their daughters in childhood. Perhaps this was merely malicious rumour; the reason given – that the breast obstructs the proper drawing of the bowstring and through its burning off all the strength goes into the right shoulder and arm – certainly does not seem very convincing.

Interpretations of the Amazon graves leaves many questions unanswered. Furthermore, those offered so far are both unsatisfactory and varied in nature.[14]. Whatever the case, it is certain that the way of life of the stock-breeding nomads of the steppe provided the best conditions for the participation of women in hunting and in contests on horseback, and in other martial contests – in all of which we may assume they took a natural pleasure.

65  *Depiction of an Amazon or barbarian on a grave stele from the vicinity of Olbia (Farmakovski). Height 25.6 in. (0.65 m). Early fifth century BC*

# 6 Episodes from everyday Scythian life

## A trader's unfortunate fate

Sometime towards the end of the fifth century BC, a young man did not return from a trading voyage into northern Scythia. His boat capsized in a minor tributary of the Dnieper, his valuable cargo – a large number of gold-plated bronze vessels – sank, and the young man perished. The river-bed gradually shifted, and the body was covered by almost 6.6 ft (2 m) of peat.

In 1962 peat-workers and archaeologists discovered the traces of this ancient misfortune near the village of Peščanoe in the Ukraine district of Zolotonosa (Oblast' Čerkassy). They found the boat, a large, simple one made from the trunk of a single oak, the skeleton of the dead boatman showing him to be a young man of the Mediterranean type, and the 15 magnificent Greek gold-plated bronze vessels which today are kept in the treasure chamber of the Cave Monastery at Kiev.

Unfortunately, we do not know whether the young man was Scythian or Greek, since the anthropological differences between the two peoples are too slight to allow positive identification. Neither do we know the exact departure point of his journey. If he had come from the north Pontic Greek towns, however, he could hardly have made the long voyage alone. He may have had a companion, who was able to save himself. But in that case the valuable cargo would presumably have been salvaged – which would no doubt have been possible. If he was indeed alone, he would have been a middleman with a 'representative' in Scythia. Unfortunately, the excavations have not provided any precise information.

The young man may have been set upon, or caught in a storm, or perhaps it was merely an error in the distribution of the load which had caused the boat to capsize....

Despite these unanswered questions, the find casts interesting new light on the trade between Greeks and Scythians, its extent and its importance. The boat was simple and functional in design. The site of the find – about 311 miles (500 km) from any Greek town – lies far to the north of the former rapids which today are buried under 131 ft (40 m) of water in the Kachova reservoir. These rapids, as mentioned earlier, presented a considerable obstacle to the navigators of antiquity for a distance of 47 miles (75 km). They are nevertheless mentioned neither by Herodotus, who was certainly familiar with the geography of the areas he dealt with, nor by any other writers. The Byzantine Emperor Constantine Porphyrogenetos, in the tenth century AD, was the first to provide any description of the rapids. Medieval merchants and soldiers could only traverse this stretch by unloading their boats and ships and transporting the cargo overland.

Owing to the lack of ancient references, some scholars have assumed that the rapids were situated at the northern edge of the world known to the Greeks. Our trading boat is a further significant indication that this assumption is erroneous. Skilful tradesmen apparently managed either to overcome this obstacle alone, or to come to a no doubt profitable arrangement with Scythian middlemen.

What was dear to Scythian hearts is clearly shown in the preserved portion of the cargo:

rich, in part magnificently decorated Greek vessels in what was at the time 'traditional' style, and fashioned with considerable skill. They included amphorae, water jugs, dishes and buckets, as well as a mixing bowl, all evidently intended for wine or wine mixtures. This function, together with the size of the vessels, fits in very well with the Scythians' almost proverbial love of wine and wild drinking bouts which was notorious throughout the ancient world.

## Scythian drinking

Come, my boy, give me the goblet,
In one draught it shall be emptied!
In the jug mix ten parts water,
Five parts wine thou shalt add to it.
I would be intoxicated,
Not gripped in maenadic frenzy.

Let us not again this evening
With our shouts and noisy uproar
Get ourselves as drunk as Scythians,
Let's get moderately tipsy
And our best songs sing with fervour.

(Anacreon, 3:43, first half of the sixth century BC.)

That Scythian drinking continued in the grave – at least in the minds of those left behind – is indicated by finds of separately constructed wine cellars with between ten and 15 wine amphorae which had indeed held wine, as shown by a reddish-brown deposit inside them. This was frequently expensive wine imported from the Greek islands, as the seals and writing on the amphorae show. The women as well as the men were keen devotees of Bacchus: well-ordered 'wine cellars' and an abundance of drinking vessels have been found in the graves of rich women.

## 'Potent milk'

The national drink of the Scythians was 'koumiss' – fermented, mildly alcoholic mare's milk. Koumiss is the typical nomad drink which owing to its very high vitamin content (especially vitamin C) provided a vital supplement to the Scythians' otherwise unrelieved diet of meat. The effects of koumiss range from a strengthening of the nervous system and stimulation of the blood formation to regulation of gastric acid, and are still appreciated today.

Wilhelm von Rubruk, a Franciscan monk sent by the Pope to the Mongols in 1253, vividly describes the revulsion and distaste which he felt on tasting koumiss for the first time. After long years of journeying he was, on his return, given a farewell audience with Baidshu, commander-in-chief of the army on the Araxes. Out of consideration he was offered wine by his host, who himself drank koumiss – 'which *I* should have preferred had I been offered it', writes the disappointed Rubruk, thus clearly indicating that it is also possible for a central European palate to acquire this taste.

## Scythian 'incense'

In his dictionary written in the fifth century AD the Greek grammarian Hesychios of Alexandria gives the word 'hemp' a synonym which translates as 'Scythian incense'. The author is referring here to a well-known episode from Herodotus.

After his impressive account of a Scythian royal burial, Herodotus describes an activity which he assumes to be a particularly effective kind of vapour bath (Book IV, 73): the Scythians crawl into little felt tents, in the middle of which are red-hot stones. On to these they throw hemp seeds, which they cultivate themselves, and inhale the smoke. Presumably the heat inside the little tents caused the participants to sweat, which Herodotus (or his informant) found particularly noteworthy.

This account reveals that the 'Father of History' had never smoked pot himself: his interpretation of events would otherwise have seemed less naïve. The fact that the Scythians 'howled with pleasure' would not have been attributed by him to their enjoyment of the 'vapour-bath'; he would have realized that they were simply high.

Ever since whole sets of hemp-inhaling equipment were found in the frozen tombs of the Altai, proving Herodotus's information to be accurate, his account has not been questioned. Evidence was found there of a culture directly related to that of the Scythians ('Altai Scythians'); it corresponds down to the last detail to the ancient description:

*Tents* approximately 4 ft (1.20 m) high constructed of a frame of six poles tied together at the top, which could be erected quickly and easily; finely decorated *felt or leather rugs* to cover the frame; *bronze cauldrons* which contained the hot stones, as can be seen from heat cracks on their surfaces. To prevent scorching, the handles of the cauldrons were thickly bound with birch bark.

A leather bag filled with hemp seeds, and more seeds among the stones, some of them charred, lead us to conclude that the 'incense' vessels were actually smouldering when the mourners left the tombs, so that the dead remained behind wreathed in hemp smoke. Besides hemp seeds (*cannabis sativa*), seeds of melilot (*melilotus*) indicate further use of intoxicants.

The question of course arises as to whether this practice had a purely ritual purpose or whether it was an everyday pleasure enjoyed by the Scythians. The ingenious interpretation that only priests indulged in hashish-inhaling during the funeral rites, can no longer be accepted with its limiting implications. Since it was clearly a matter of course for both men and women to be buried equipped with working apparatus for hemp-inhaling, it is obvious that this intoxicant was also used deliberately for non-religious purposes. The inhaling of hashish – pure hemp seeds at that! – with its manifold effects such as time distortion and the deadening of pain could, amongst other things, have been a useful substance to take during preparations for battle.

We know from written sources that the Thracians, from the country bordering on the west of Scythia, went into battle under the influence of intoxicants. A neighbouring tribe on the eastern border – the *saka haumavarga* ('hauma-drinking' Sakas) – probably used

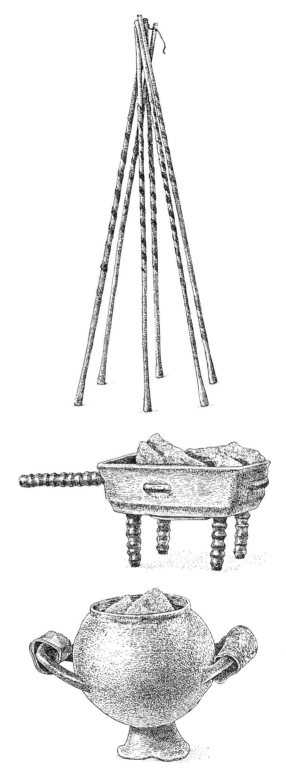

66 *Hemp-inhaling equipment from the Pazyryk kurgans (Artamanov).*

fly agaric sediment which may have had intoxicating effects similar to the frenzy of the berserker. Reports of hemp-growing came from Scythia itself, and we know of miniature tents found in the Altai, complete with the necessary burning equipment. It is clear that the modern stigma attached to drug-taking did not apply in antiquity, and their use before battle (similar to that of the later 'assassins'[15]) may have played an important role, possibly even contributing to victory.

## Scythian 'minstrels'

The Scythians and their northerly neighbours, the Androphagi, Melanchlaeni and Arimaspians, played flutes made from eagle and vulture bones, as we know from written accounts. Archaeological finds have confirmed this: we have at least one definite find (from mound 5 in Skatovka, in the lower Volga region) of pan-pipes made from the bones of birds' feet. Present-day Bulgarian folk instruments show that the tone of flutes made from the bones of birds of prey is of a particular quality – gentle but rich and intense.

Their music was not confined to pan-pipes, however. There are several representations of Scythians playing lyres, among which is a depiction from the fourth century BC on a broad gold-foil headband. It is a festive scene with a woman sitting in state as its centrepiece and various other figures arranged on her right and left. On her left a musician is kneeling with a lyre. C. Strauss, who has researched into the musical instruments of Eurasian horse-riding nomads, has discovered striking similarities to later Germanic lyres of the sixth and seventh centuries AD that we know from the 'singer's tomb' in Cologne and from Oberflacht in Würtemberg.

To all appearances we have here a lyre player who is playing for a festive occasion at court. The fingers of his left hand are playing on the strings, or at least touching them. His face has a soulful expression and he seems totally immersed in his instrument. The slightly parted lips may possibly even indicate that the singer is performing a Scythian equi-

67 *Bearded Scythian playing the lyre, on a headband from the kurgan of Sachnovka (from a photograph by Kločko).*

valent of the *Nibelungenlied*.

According to literary sources, plectrums made from goats' hooves were used, and it is therefore possible that in future excavations we may find indirect evidence of instruments in Scythian graves despite the fact that soil conditions have not favoured the preservation of the highly sensitive instruments themselves.

## In the Scythian gaming room

A find from the far-off (yet culturally closely-related) Altai reveals an interesting pastime of the inhabitants of the steppe. It is a multi-coloured carpet 6 × 6.6 ft (1.80 x 2 m) in size. Its discovery caused a considerable stir, not only owing to its early date (fifth century BC) but mainly because of the quality of the hand-knotting. The amount of work involved, as calculated by experts, is one of the most impressive things about the carpet. It has a short pile and is closely woven, consisting of 1,250,000 knots of the 'Turkish' kind. From calculations based on the daily quota of the most skilful weavers today (2000 to 3000 knots), this carpet must have taken about 500 working days to complete. The colours used range from dark red, orange and bright yellow through blue and green to black and white. The pattern corresponds to that of oriental carpets, having a large central section and five surrounding bands.

Of particular interest is the wide outer band. Since the original is damaged at one corner, we cannot be certain whether 15 men are riding and 13 walking or whether the proportion was exactly 14 to 14. The horses are proceeding from left to right. The riders, either astride the animals or leading them, wear typical nomad dress. The horses are heavily-built greys and show a remarkable

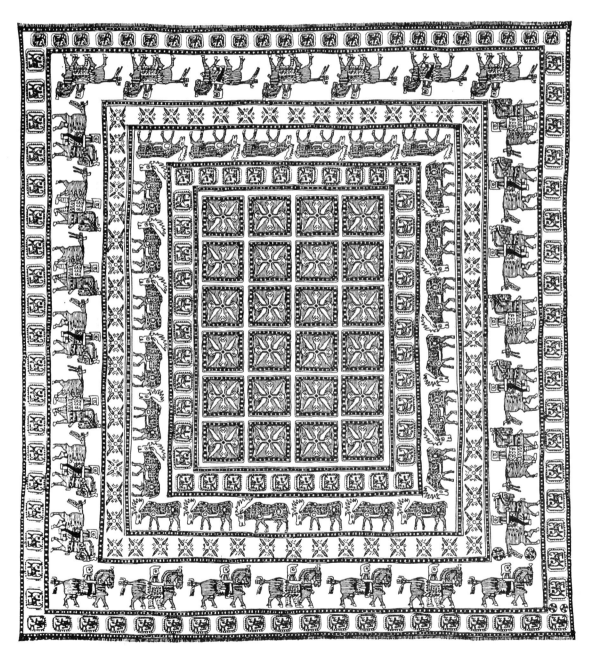

resemblance to the 'Persepolis ponies' – the horses on the famous Achaemenid relief in Persepolis. They are all clearly shown to be stallions, and pacing; they wear show harness and saddle-cloths and their manes have been clipped to stand rigid. Their tails have been knotted and their head-hair plumed. The saddle-cloths are particularly attractive; they are clearly differentiated by colour and design as if the animals were from several stud farms or the riders from competing clubs.

A significant observation has been made by J. Wiesner: at one of the outer corners (here bottom right) there are two round marks which have a parallel, though of a different design, in the rider frieze. These probably marked the point where the game began.

We know of richly inlaid game boards from

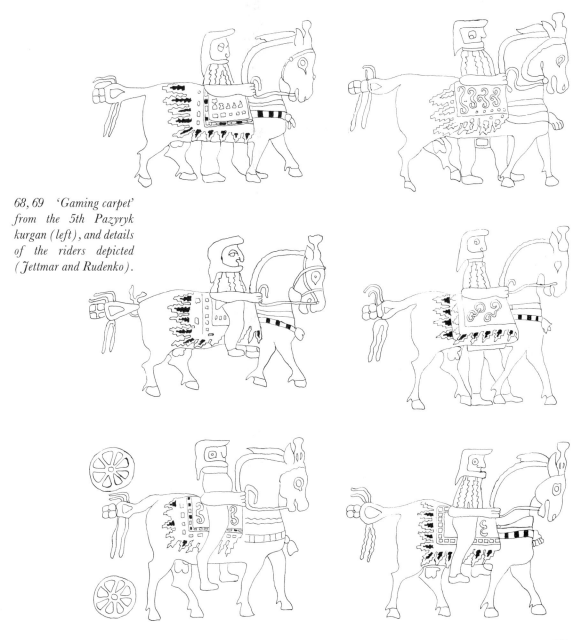

*68, 69  'Gaming carpet' from the 5th Pazyryk kurgan (left), and details of the riders depicted (Jettmar and Rudenko).*

the famous shaft graves of Ur (Mesopotamia) dating from the third millennium BC. They were to provide amusement for the dead in the next world, and were decorated with what were clearly allegorical animal depictions. Although the finds in Ur also include the pieces used in the games, we know nothing of the rules. The same applies to the 'gaming carpet' from the Pazyryk kurgan. We have no idea how the game started or whether they played with dice or with small bones taken from sheeps' ankle-joints, popular objects resembling polished ivory which are found in many graves. We do not know how the game was won or lost, or whether only one game could be played on the carpet or several (as draughts and chess can be played on the same board today). At all events this 'gaming board' was extremely practical and could also be used as a floor covering, wall hanging or blanket, as well as being easily transportable on horseback.

We can imagine how in the harsh steppe winter, with icy winds blowing round the yurts and other dwellings, the oil lamps and fires – not to mention the wine and milk schnaps – would provide the Scythians with warmth. It may be that the atmosphere was not always so idyllic, that sometimes the players sitting round the carpet (possibly including women) would be carried away in the heat of the game, and gamble away a particularly spirited horse, a beautiful woman taken prisoner in war or even everything they possessed (as Tacitus so vividly reports of the Germanic tribes) . . . .

## *Buskashi* in antiquity?

We have little information concerning Scythian games and sport. In addition to wrestling and probably boxing matches, contests in various weapon skills would ensure that the warriors were physically fit for the campaigns ahead. The riding contests would presumably have played a central role, with their testing of various skills which today are only seen – if at all – in the circus arena or as display interludes at riding events. Such skills would include standing on a galloping horse, jumping over several animals, changing riders at full speed, lassoing games and much else besides.

A Scythian national sport of particular interest was the spearing of hares from horseback. It is known to us through pictorial representation and from written sources. The rules were simple: the riders tried to kill the hare at full gallop with a lance or short spear. To make it more difficult they used very short or even broken off lances, which were perhaps hurled – the depictions leave this last question open. At all events this hunting sport required of the horse the skills of a hunting dog, and great determination on the part of the rider in holding on to his prey which the other riders would probably try to wrest from him. The Scythians were so fond of this sport that they would drop everything else in order to indulge in it, as an episode from Herodotus's Book IV illustrates with unintended humour. Herodotus writes that during the Persian invasion under Darius (513/12 BC) after much toing and froing there was finally a battle line-up of the two armies. Shortly before the battle was due to begin, a hare suddenly ran through the rows of Scythians under their King, Idanthyrsus, and the warriors began to chase it, causing the Scythian ranks to break. We are told that Darius, who had been longing for a pitched battle in order to end the unsuccessful and difficult campaign without too much loss of face, asked in surprise what was causing the commotion on the other side. On being told the reason, he is said to have felt so deeply humiliated at not being taken seriously and so demoralized by the unconcealed self-assurance of the Scythians that he ordered his army to retreat.

Anyone familiar with the horse-riding sports of the Asiatic steppes knows the passion and enthusiasm with which they are practised even today. Galloping along on the hunt the riders become oblivious to their surroundings, the masses of horses are practically on top of one another, the drumming of the hooves is all-pervading, and the body of the animal they have been chasing is finally so mutilated that it is difficult to tell who has actually won.

The 'hare chase' of the Scythians seems to have presented the dismayed Darius with a spectacle similar to the *buskashi*, the rough, reckless horse-riding sport involving a dead goat or calf in which up to a thousand riders participate even today in central Asia.

*70, 71   Gold plaques from the Kul'-Oba kurgan (Artamonov).*

# 7 Animal husbandry, household and settlement

## Composition of the herds

The rhythm of life in the vast Scythian steppes was determined by the huge herds, filling the air with their noises. The lives of the inhabitants of the steppes revolved around these animals: they had to be looked after and provided for. Nomadic dependence on livestock meant that huge areas of pastureland were required, in order to avoid overgrazing and overmanuring, which would lead to the destruction of the turf. Right up until the last century therefore, it was a sign of poverty if nomads were to settle, not a voluntary change over to a more 'civilized' life. In the spring, when the steppe was covered in lush green, the feeding of even large herds presented no difficulty. In summer, however, when a scorching sun had left only dried-up yellowish brown patches, the provision of food and water became a matter of life and death requiring organization and security of property, failing which they had to acquire pasture by force.

Theories concerning stocks of domesticated and wild animals in Scythian times can be supported by a large quantity of animal bones which have been unearthed in systematic excavations and scientifically analysed. Foremost in this field are V.I. Calkins and his group, whose scholarly works provide fundamental analyses, with presentation and interpretation of the material. Calkins's first major study, in 1960, was already based on an examination of 320,000 bones of 12,500 animals from the Scythian region of the steppes.

Livestock-rearing in the region north of the Black Sea reached a very high standard in the late Bronze Age. The tribes of the late Bronze Age, including the Cimmerians, the predecessors of the Scythians, bred cattle, sheep, goats, pigs and horses. It seems that they also knew of camels, although these were apparently of no significance to them. The early Iron Age brought with it no new animal species apart from the domestic cat and the donkey, which appeared during the course of the Greek colonization on the coastal strip of the Black Sea. The proportion of one species to another changed completely, however.

Studies of the composition of the herds in the two periods show quite differing emphases. In the first millennium BC a change in the size of domesticated animals can be observed which appears to affect all species: the animals become smaller, cattle and horses for example by as much as 2 in. (5 cm) in the height of the withers, no mean amount considering that average sizes in Scythian times were already small (cows 43 in. (109 cm), bulls 44 in. (112 cm) and oxen 48 in. (123 cm) in wither height). The reasons for this gradual reduction in size are not yet clear and are still being debated. So far, a similar process to that in Europe as a whole can be discerned, which is characterized by a continuous decrease in the size of domesticated species since neolithic times. This development was intensified in eastern Europe in the early Iron Age but did not reach its peak until the Middle Ages; in modern times there has been an increase in the growth rate. Whether the reasons for the decrease in size lay in the way the animals were kept and fed, or whether it was caused by a radical worsening of the climate and similar factors, are questions which must remain open for the time being.

At the same time a change in the kind of animals kept can be clearly observed. The predominance of cattle still evident in the Bronze Age was replaced in Scythian times by that of sheep, while the horse became increasingly important – unmistakable features of the nomadic life style. The keeping of pigs was confined to the forest steppe region and thus to the areas inhabited by settled or semi-settled tribes.

Palaeozoological evidence gives concrete support to an assertion of Herodotus which has evoked smiles of incredulity and the suspicion that the 'Father of History' had had his leg pulled by foreigners in distant countries. In Book IV, 29, Herodotus states that the Scythian cattle had no horns, a condition which he attributed to the extreme cold. Modern research has confirmed this observation of 'hornless cattle'. The breeds of cattle in the region north of the Black Sea at this time were indeed predominantly hornless or very short-horned. It is noticeable that these new breeds only appeared at the time of the Scythian immigration; it seems clear that they must have brought them from their old homelands in the east.

## Red horses, golden riders

The most important and versatile animal in Scythian times was without doubt the horse. It provided not only meat, which was cooked in many different ways, but also the milk from which butter, cheese and in particular koumiss, were produced. Furthermore the horse was used for riding and as a beast of burden, and directed by a skilful rider to bite and kick could even become a 'weapon' in battle. There are numerous accounts of the close attachment of the Scythians to their horses – and also of the horses to them.

As far as we can tell from depictions from the fifth to the third century BC, the Scythians preferred to ride stallions. Pliny does however mention later, in his *Natural History* (8, 165), that they favoured mares in battle, as they 'can urinate while galloping', a natural ability denied to geldings and stallions for which that operation is a more complicated affair. Pliny's remark brings to mind the famous fighting mares of the Arabs. Strabo (VII, 4,8) informs us in addition that the stallions were castrated in order to render them 'gentler', since the animals were small, he says, but very fast and spirited. This may have contributed significantly to the orderliness and docility of the herds, but the preference for stallions evident in the depictions, at least as steeds for the men, is consistent with the required 'equality' of horse and rider which is considered vital in the Caucasian-Iranian region even today.

The preference for stallions is understandable, as the natural display pattern of an animal which has not been castrated can develop impressively under a good rider. The Scythians, riding without stirrups and with only light saddles or saddle-cloths, their legs clasping the animal low on its belly, present a very harmonious picture in which man and beast merge into a single whole.

Many peoples of antiquity and medieval times, even right up to the modern age, chose not to castrate their young stallions and so deprive them of vigour and those characteristics which are partly pleasant and partly unpleasant for the rider. Only modern civilization with its denseness of settlement and traffic, and the destruction of the inherited natural environment, has created the modern 'equestrian' whose preference is for the gelding and the riding arena. In Scythian times such things were inconceivable.

Considerable information as to the appearance, size, coat colour and other features of Scythian horses has been derived from archaeological material. Compared with present-day crossbreeds they were small and slight in build. According to finds so far discovered the largest horses had a withers height of between 58.3 and 59 in. (148 and 150 cm), occasionally between 59 and 63 in. (150 and 160 cm). Nevertheless they were among the largest horses of the time and were far above the average height of Celtic and Germanic horses. From the present-day point of view their size corresponds to pure-bred

*72   Detail from the pectoral, colour plate 14. Milking a sheep (Photo: Kločko).*

*73   Portrayal of a cow. Horns are rare in animals from the Scythian region (Photo: Kločko).*

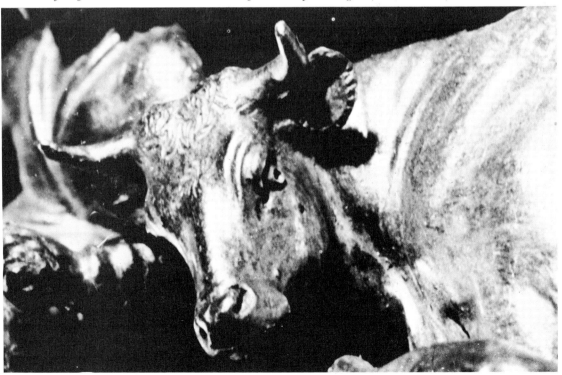

Arab horses, which the finest among them resembled. Since according to ancient sources the Scythian breeders were also familiar with the device of controlled incest (crossing of particularly fine mares with their stallion sons) this parallel is not surprising. The high standard of Scythian horse-breeding is also demonstrated by an incident which occurred after the devastating military defeat of the old Scythian King, Ateas, at the hands of Philip II of Macedonia in 339 BC. Philip, father of Alexander the Great, is said to have chosen 20,000 thoroughbred mares from the spoils, in order to improve the stock of Macedonian horses. He had overreached himself, however, for on the march back the huge herd was taken from him by recalcitrant tribes.

According to archaeological finds, there were at least three different breeds of horse in European Scythia, of which the working horse and the well-trained thoroughbred fighting horse are depicted on the famous Čertomlyk amphora.

This is the showpiece from an excavation made shortly after the middle of the nineteenth century in the royal burial mound of Čertomlyk – the largest of all Scythian burial mounds. The 27.6 in. (70 cm) high silver vessel was discovered in the Queen's chamber. The amphora, in part thickly gilded, has a sculptured frieze round its top half, of extraordinarily vivid individually moulded figures in high relief which had been later welded on, showing the Scythians involved in various activities with their horses. This magnificent vessel was probably intended for wine, since sieves had been fitted into the three spouts in the shape of animal heads at the bottom and into the neck at the top. Furthermore, not only was this vessel found near the sarcophagus, but a whole wine supply together with the sacrificed cup-bearer was also found.

The individual motifs of this frieze are breaking in, training, and catching and releasing the animals in pasture. In the centre of the display side three people are trying to

*74 Young Scythian man or woman sealing a vessel filled with milk, a Greek wine amphora (Photo: Kločko).*

*75 Head of a mare turned towards her suckling foal (Photo: Kločko).*

train a horse to kneel down. Unfortunately only traces remain of the ropes (in the form of small silver chains) which they held in their hands. This particular training was very important in battle, as kneeling on command could mean the difference between life and death for a fallen and heavily-armed warrior, relatively immobile on foot, who could save time getting swiftly back on his kneeling horse, stirrups being unknown at the time. This important motif is even part of the decoration on a royal golden neck ring, whose end figures are Scythians seated on their kneeling horses.

Training horses to kneel down was a custom peculiar to the nomadic peoples and not practised among the Greeks. If it had been, Xenophon would not have left us such exquisite instructions on the mounting of a horse – by clutching the mane or using the lance in a kind of pole-vault in order to catapult oneself into the saddle. He lays particular emphasis on 'posture'! The ancient author warns that the rider might otherwise present an 'indecent sight' from behind (since trousers were unknown to the Greeks).

Bukephalos too, the famous Thessalian fighting horse of Alexander the Great, who is said to have mastered the skill of kneeling down, probably had in his youth a similar training to the Čertomlyk horses. The small bone-carving illustrated here, with a Scythian obviously having been dragged to the ground, shows that the training and harnessing of these self-willed animals did not always proceed smoothly.

On the left of the central scene on the Čertomlyk amphora, an older Scythian is training a magnificent, bridled stallion to

*78 Carving on an ivory plaque from the Kul'-Oba kurgan (Grakov).*

bend its leg slowly; this probably enabled the rider to mount the horse in a particularly elegant way. The Scythian on the far right, on the other hand, is tying his horse's front legs together, leaving it to pasture with saddle-strap unfastened. This last animal differs from the others in the inferior shape of its head and the relative ungainliness of its body. It is very reminiscent of a wild horse of the Tarpan or Przewalski type, and probably represents the riding beast of the common people.

The Scythian horses were kept in herds which might be described as 'mobile stud-farms'. Even as late as the nineteenth century

*76 The two ends of the gold neck ring from the Kul'-Oba kurgan (Antiquités du Bosphore Cimmerien).*

*77 Frieze on the silver amphora (Drevnosti Gerodotovoi Skifii).*

this kind of horse-rearing was usual in the southern part of the Russian Empire. It was only in winter that the animals were put into pens or stables; for long periods during the rest of the year they were left either in the charge of their herdsmen, the *tabunchiks*, or to themselves. In the nineteenth century, such a herd or *tabun* usually consisted of a thousand horses, of which between 15 and 20 were stallions, 400 to 500 were breeding mares and between 500 and 600 were foals and geldings.

'Truly, the soul of such a herdsman must be as tough as leather! He is clothed from head to foot in it as well', was Kohl's description of the last 'Scythians' in 1841. Great skill and experience were necessary to keep such a herd together, and he adds the following remarks on the day's work of a *tabunchik*:

'The restless temperament of the animals in his charge allows him not a moment's peace. The thousand horses in his *tabun* do not keep together like a regiment of dragoons, and in order to signal to them his commands he has to ride in front of his ranks more often every day than an adjutant in battle. He lives day and night on his horse, which is not only his chair but also his table, his couch and his bed.'[16]

Anyone wanting a vivid impression of Scythian horses will find the descriptions of these *tabun* horses very useful. We read, for instance, of their skilful fights against steppe wolves, which they 'stamped level with the ground', and of the 'personalities' of the leader stallions with their fully developed natural characteristics. A description of the difficulties arising when two *tabuns* met, conjures up an atmosphere which can without doubt be transposed back into Scythian times:

'They shake their flowing manes, and their hooves of horn clash together in the air like shields. At the same time they emit whistling, shrieking and roaring noises such as we have never experienced coming from our own well-tamed horses and which might be compared to the howling of wild animals rather than to the neighing of our horses.'[17]

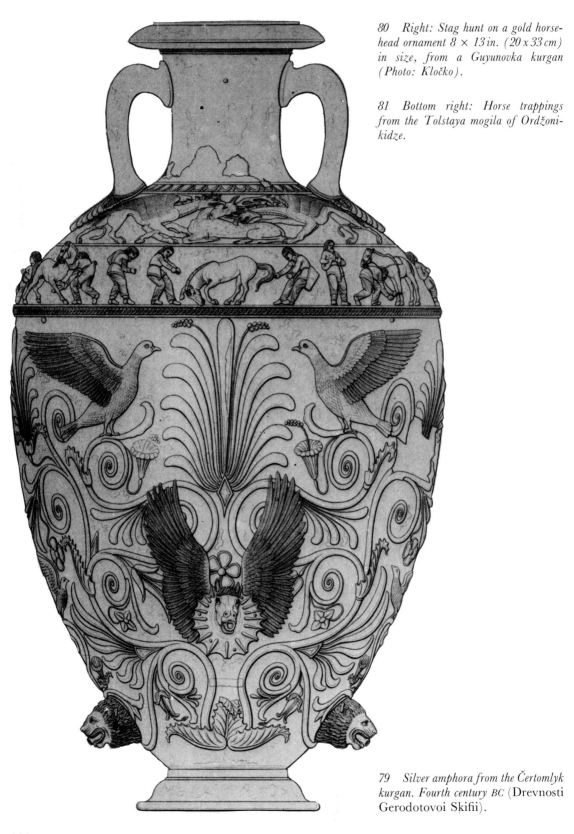

80 Right: Stag hunt on a gold horse-head ornament 8 × 13 in. (20 x 33 cm) in size, from a Guyunovka kurgan (Photo: Kločko).

81 Bottom right: Horse trappings from the Tolstaya mogila of Ordžoni-kidze.

79 Silver amphora from the Čertomlyk kurgan. Fourth century BC (Drevnosti Gerodotovoi Skifii).

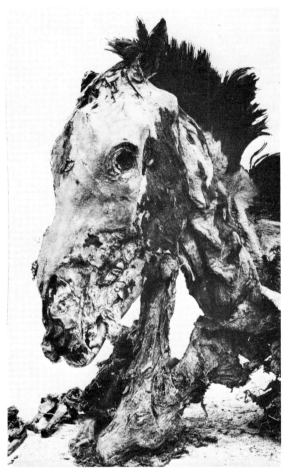

82   Horses from the Pazyryk kurgans after excavation
(Photo: Griaznov). The animals were in such a good
state of preservation that osteological and craniological
examinations were possible, as well as analyses of skin,
coat, musculature and even stomach contents.

Throughout the whole of the Scythian-Sakan region, as far as the Altai, there was a preference for reddish-brown horses. Only bays or chestnuts were used for riding, and animals with white markings were rejected. This may have been for practical reasons, as the hoof horn of horses with white fetlocks is still held today to be more fragile, an important factor at a time when the horseshoe was unknown and especially in areas of rough terrain. The particular preference for reddish-coloured ('flame-coloured') horses among the ancient peoples of the steppe belt as far as India, is seen by many authors as connected with sun worship. And it is doubtless no coincidence that horses were also sacrificed to the sun.

The 'horse mummies' from the Pazyryk kurgans in the Altai have yielded a considerable amount of information; even the contents of the stomachs with the remains of their feed could be analysed. The Altai and the areas on its eastern borders are rough, inhospitable regions which for many reasons would have been extremely unsuitable for horse-breeding. The well-developed horses found in the Altai kurgans must therefore have been imported. This also explains the high regard in which they were held. The investigations showed that the tallest animals were often also the oldest – between 18 and 20 or more – when they were killed with a blow to the forehead and placed in the grave for their dead master. The question of where the 'Pazyrykers' got their magnificent horses focuses our attention on the regions bordering the Altai on the west, which had always been the natural habitat of famous breeds of horses. The nearest parallel to the Pazyryk horses in type may thus be seen in the horses of the Achal-Tekke region, which are known for their toughness and stamina. The reconstructions shown between pages 64–5 are based on the concrete example of one single burial of a rich Altai dweller (kurgan 1), and illustrate the extent of the material wealth represented by such burial offerings, which have for the most part survived only as insignificant-looking bone remains and a few traces of paint and leather.

The opulence of the harness decoration corresponded to the wealth and nobility of the rider. The brow and the area of the horse's head between the brow and the nose, the cheek straps, blinkers, and any of the cross-straps on the bridle part of the halter including the reins could be decorated with gold. On the basis of finds unearthed so far, it seems that few riders, perhaps only those of the highest social ranks, were entitled to ride with a saddle decorated with gold. In addition to the gleam of the gold ornamentation and the warm yellow and red of the horses' coats, there were brightly painted saddles, leather trappings decorated with embroidery and appliqué, boars' tusks pierced through and other similar amulets, bells, half-moons and other ornaments together with the scalps of vanquished foes fixed to the leather trappings of the horse. The animals' tails were carefully dressed, and in order to remove any obstacle to using the bow the manes were cut short. A few longer tufts were left on the withers to give the riders, who rode without stirrups, some extra stability.

The rich warriors on their gleaming red animals, with shining gold clothing and weapons, must have presented an impressive picture in the brilliant sunlight of the steppe. 'Golden' riders on red horses doubtless also peopled the Scythian 'Valhalla'.

As late as the Middle Ages it was part of the military strategy of the nomads who reared livestock to drive part of their herds into enemy territory at the outbreak of hostilities – as a gesture of mockery and contempt – and to let them pasture there and drink the enemy's water. The attacking Polovci for instance, in the eleventh and twelfth centuries, first made themselves known to the inhabitants of old Kiev through their herds, which from the high walls would have appeared as a 'feeding' siege encircling the city. The waggons and felt tents of the Polovci then followed as the next step in the escalation. An episode from Frontinus's treatise on military strategies indicates that procedures were similar in ancient times. The Scythian King Ateas, involved in clashes with the Triballian tribes, as a last resort directed the women and children to drive the animals towards the enemy lines. The Triballians thought that Ateas had had reinforcements from other Scythian tribes and put an end to hostilities.


## Cultivated plants

Whereas livestock-breeding was prevalent in the southern region of the steppe, agriculture and horticulture were well developed in the forest steppe to the north. Conditions here were favourable for this, since the forest steppe lies in the zone of moderately humid, very fertile soil consisting of various kinds of black earth. Because of this, agriculture in the area had ancient beginnings and can be traced as far back as the fourth millennium BC as an important means of subsistence.

Recent pollen analysis suggests that the forest steppe was already forming in palaeolithic times. It was apparently not a case of the steppe advancing northwards, but rather of an extension southwards of the forest. In the transition from the second to the first millennium BC, this led to the final emergence of a forest steppe belt several hundred miles wide. Parallel with this came a clear climatic deterioration – it became colder and damper.

In Scythian times the forest steppe and the steppe comprised a single political unit. The forest steppe was the home of the agricultural Scythians, and of related tribes assumed to be of different ethnic origin who had been conquered by the invading nomads. Through them the forest steppe became the 'granary' of the nomad princes, who as trade magnates were the economic exploiters of the corn trade with Greece, no doubt the source of the enormous riches which filled the tombs of the nomadic nobility. Against this background the intense Scythianization of the forest steppe can be readily comprehended. The question of the cultural, ethnic and especially linguistic background to this process still presents a scientific problem which makes it impossible for us to establish the northern boundary of Scythia for certain. For understandable reasons some scholars would like to see in certain of the forest steppe tribes the ancestors of the Slavs, although this hypothesis is today held to be highly improbable.

There is evidence of an abundance of cultivated plants in Scythian times. As well as several well-cultivated types of wheat, they grew barley, millet, rye and seed oats, possibly also buckwheat, of which there are indications not yet fully substantiated. In addition there was a considerable number of pulses such as peas, lentils, sweet peas, beans and broad beans, and also rape, flax and hemp. Huge masses of weeds grew amongst the cultivated plants. The wheat varieties proved on analysis to be of such high quality that the extensive wheat exports to Greece can be readily understood. On the other hand the evidence from the north Pontic Greek cities so far indicates the presence of only hard wheat, a comparatively primitive variety. There are literary references to onions and sweet 'Scythian roots', and some authors have taken this to be a poetic term for the radish, although this is not very convincing. In recent years indications of horticulture have been increasing. The charred pips of apples and cherries verify their cultivation; drying ovens for fruit show a kind of preserving system which is still in use today. In addition, hazelnuts and acorns were gathered. Sickles and scythes were used to reap the harvest, which was kept in large grain pits in the settlements.

A completely unexpected source of information on palaeolithic plant cultivation is found in clay models of pulses and corn discovered on sacrificial sites in considerable numbers in modern forest steppe excavations: exact 'copies' of wheat, barley, rye, peas and chick-peas, as well as sweet peas and millet. These places of sacrifice were altars for burning, carefully formed out of clay, and the thick layers of ash and animal bones on their decorated surfaces are evidence of animal sacrifice. Round the edges, or at least in the immediate vicinity, there are often artisan or agricultural and herding deposits in the form of implements and semi-finished products or the clay 'grain' mentioned above, together with a large number of small animal figurines. When the clay corn models were analysed they showed variations in the X-ray results, which proved under the microscope to be caused by structural differences in the manufacturing material. The basic material for the models was always clay, but flour from the appropriate cereal was also added. Since flour could be only coarsely ground with the hand-grinders of the time, husks of the various cereals can still clearly be seen on the photographic enlargements, making identification easy.

There is as yet no explanation for this 'cereal cult'. They were certainly not trying to deceive the gods with their imitations; this is belied by the amount of work involved and the unusual care with which the models were fashioned and which indicates that there was actually a craft for the production of 'devotional objects'. Artificial cereal grains and animal figurines probably constituted only part of the products of this craft which the faithful offered up to gain the favour of the gods during cult activities and processions. It is possible that their hope for a good harvest or other aspects of fertility played a part here.

*83   View of the household niche in the Gaymanova mogila (Bidzilya).*

*84   Household area with vessels for supplies of wine, and the skeleton of a sacrificed serving girl in the Melitopol'
kurgan ( Pokrovskaya and Terenožkin ).*

*85   The excavator Veselovski in 1913 with the finds from the household area of the Solocha kurgan. See fig. 47
( Brašinski ).*

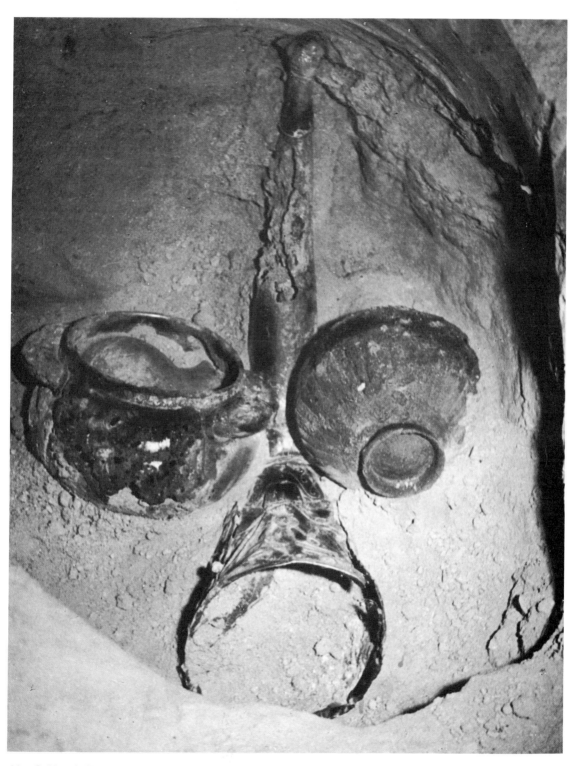

*86   Gold and silver drinking vessels in the 'hiding-place' in the Gaymanova mogila, see p. 57f. (Bidzilya).*

## The Scythian kitchen

Animal bones and other kitchen refuse, household sections and kitchen alcoves in the tombs provide a fairly precise idea of the Scythian menu and indicate a love of food and drink in abundance. We can visualize the interior of a Scythian kitchen from the example of the kitchen niche in the Gaymanova burial mound, which was found intact. Bronze cauldrons of different sizes are immediately noticeable. These are extremely typical and were intended for meat portions of considerable size. Their capacity – up to 31 gallons (140 litres) – was large enough for a whole butchered foal. Mutton would be cooked in smaller cauldrons. The Gaymanova mogila also contained a portable bronze stove with two handles, whose cylindrical hollow base could be placed on red-hot coals – up to now a unique find. We can only admire the practical and manageable design of this little steppe oven: in the cold season it provided warmth and at the same time could be used for frying, roasting or boiling and for heating up smaller portions. On its grill plate lay iron rods with movable handles, no doubt forerunners of our gridirons; a utensil similar to a waffle iron was probably used for deep-fried pastries.

## Cities on wheels

In Scythia anyone possessing only one waggon was considered poor. The owner was called an 'eight-footer' after the legs of his two horses. A rich Scythian owned about 80 such waggons, as we gather from a story by Lucian. Even this is paltry compared to the 'waggon parks' of the medieval nomads.

Large numbers of waggons are also found in Scythian tombs, no doubt for the purpose of transporting the dead into the next world. So far those found had almost always been dismantled, which was probably because of ideas of the dead reawakening and fears of consequent disaster. The archaeological processing of the many finds leaves much to be desired; but we do have ancient depictions

87 *Clay models of Scythian waggon types.*

114

and clay models which convey an idea of nomadic travelling and living waggons. The models were clearly very popular as ancient toys – like the toy cars of today.

The illustrations show waggons of varying design. Large sections of the Scythian population would travel in the warmer season from one pasture to another on conveyances of this or similar kind, as verified repeatedly in written sources:

> '... people who have built neither cities nor walls, who take their dwellings with them and are without exception archers on horseback, dependent for food not on agriculture but on livestock-breeding and whose homes are their waggons – how could such a people not be invincible and difficult to corner!' (Herodotus, IV, 46)

Many ancient authors emphasized this unsettled way of life as especially typical, yet in fact it represented only one aspect of the life of horse-riding nomads, since in winter it was only possible in certain conditions. The reporters of antiquity were presumably appalled not only by this caravan life but also by the exotic sight the conveyances presented. Aeschylus, in his *Prometheus Bound*, calls them 'basketwork huts, high up on wheels, like waggons'.

A glance at the models illustrated, with their peculiar form, and a comparison with Eurasian ethnology, help to account for the disapproval of the ancient world. Several of these waggon types must have been ingenious combinations of waggons and felt yurts or tents. The upper part of the mobile base could then be lifted off when they set up camp, and put up as a yurt or tent, as was later the practice of the Tatars and Mongols. A waggon find from the Pazyryk kurgan No. 5 shows another interesting variation. This waggon, with its 8.7 ft (2.65 m) high coachwork, could be completely dismantled and thus transported on horseback along difficult mountain tracks until the waggon journey could be resumed. In Pazyryk a team of four horses was placed with the waggon – a Rolls Royce of the Altai, since as a rule the waggons were drawn by teams of oxen. Yoked oxen have a greater draught capacity than horses, whose windpipes are blocked by the brow and neck yoke, or rather their throat straps, if they are required to pull heavy loads. Since traces were unknown in the ancient world and consequently horses were also yoked, they could not be used for heavy transport even though the Scythians tried to solve the problem with an early form of horse collar; we may assume that horses were only used to pull the lighter types of waggon.

The tempo of the ox-drawn waggons doubtless synchronized with the grazing speed of the herds. M.P. Griaznov, who analysed medieval and ethnological parallel examples in order to reconstruct the life of ancient horse-riding nomads, developed the idea of a 'permanent nomadic existence' which, with certain qualifications, could also apply to Scythia. Starting from the precise account of the Franciscan Wilhelm von Rubruk, who spent a considerable time in the pasture areas of the Golden Horde of Genghis Khan's grandson Batu Khan, whose herds at that time grazed on the eastern banks of the Volga, Griaznov examined the grazing rotation. He calculated that the distance covered would have been not less than 3 miles (5 km) and not more than 5 miles (8 km) a day, amounting to about 186 miles (300 km) over five weeks. The route ran northwards from January to August, and from August onwards in the opposite direction. The horde of Sartach, Batu Khan's son, took a similar route along the west bank of the Volga.

In Mongol times the leaders and their wives travelled with hundreds, sometimes even several thousand waggons and magnificently equipped felt yurts, with all their furnishings. These were carefully set up at the places of encampment, forming portable 'palaces'. It is no wonder therefore that European travellers compared these huge gatherings to cities: 'cities on wheels' was Griaznov's apt description. Constant movement along a precisely fixed route has been noted among many nomadic peoples in whose culture caravans play an important part, so that such models are presumably applicable to the Scythians (or at least to sections of the population).

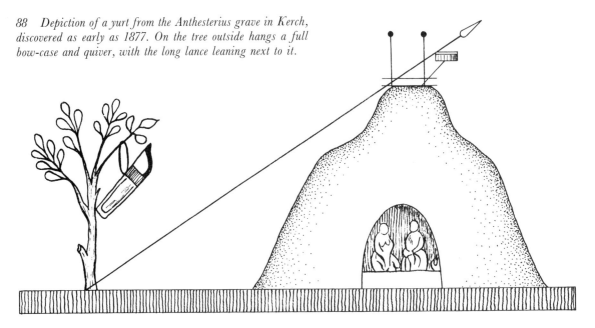

Owing to archaeological finds relating to settlement and in consideration of climatic conditions in the north Pontic steppes, other variants of nomadic life have to be taken into account, especially such forms where winter camps and fixed population centres are important.

A wall-painting from a tomb of a slightly later date (above) shows how the yurts of Scythian times might have looked. The 'master of the house' is sitting facing the entrance, ready to receive guests, as was generally the nomadic custom later on. His quiver and bowcase hangs in a tree outside, his long lance leaning next to it. No doubt life in a yurt was not to everybody's taste. From ancient times up to the Middle Ages, views expressing criticism and even revulsion at the steppe peoples and their way of life came not only from the west but also from the east, from Chinese sources. In the face of military threats from their northern neighbours, many Chinese potentates married off princesses or other high-ranking women (together with rich dowries) to leaders of the horse-riding nomads in order to secure the latter's good behaviour and loyalty. Mournful letters, indeed whole books express in poetic form the sufferings of these poor women living in barbarian exile. The change from a comfortable Chinese brick palace to a world of leather tents and felt yurts must have seemed exceedingly harsh.

Alas! in a tent
Live I now,
With felt
For walls
My food is
Only meat,
Koumiss as well
Must I drink.
Oh! my heart has been burning
Since I came,
My home my only
Constant thought.
A yellow crane
Would I be,
And swiftly fly back
To my country.

Thus mourned Hsi-chun, who had been married off in 110 BC to K'un Mo, the old ruler of the Wu-sun. And the unfortunate Wen-chi, married into the Hsiung-nu, whose leader she bore two sons, also lamented her fate and wished she had never been born.

On the other hand we find examples of nomads in completely alien cultural surroundings holding fast to their living traditions and preferring the light and airy yurts, at least in the warmer season. As evidence to support this, Soviet ethnologists investigating a modern kolkhoz in Kara-Kalpak not far from the Aral Sea in 1954 discovered the idyll illustrated below: an entire yurt, erected in a new building. And when the first Mongol became ruler of China, white mares grazed outside his palace, so that he could still enjoy his accustomed drink of koumiss, as Marco Polo reports.

## The mysterious city of Gelonus – the *gorodišče* of Bel'sk?

Far into the Scythian hinterland, reports Herodotus (the first mention of it in ancient times), lies a large city called Gelonus. It is surrounded, he says, by wooden walls 30 furlongs long each way. It has numerous wooden altars and is inhabited by the Geloni, a people of mixed Greek and Budini blood speaking the Scythian language. When the Persian army under Darius approached, the populace are said to have abandoned the city, which fell into their hands and was burned down by the Persians. Later authors of antiquity also tell of this mysterious city in the heart of Scythian country. Its name appears in various forms, and archaeologists are still searching for it today.

During the last two decades evidence has been accumulating of large numbers of fortifications and several large and diverse settlements in Scythia, which are beginning to acquire the definition 'cities' or 'city-like settlements'.

Today we know of more than a hundred of these fortified settlements (*gorodišče* in Russian) in the forest steppe region, and often their systems of fortification are very complex. Typical of these are the wood-and-earth ramparts; pointed wooden posts rammed into the ditches round the walls indicate further defence measures. The construction of the gates, which operated through an elaborate pincer mechanism, is of particular interest. The gate entrances, up to 33 ft (10 m) wide, were filled with stones at the approach of an enemy. In several of these fortified settlements one is struck by the hugeness of the interior, the fortification of an area of higher ground after the manner of an 'acropolis', the dense population and the abundance of imported goods. Soviet archaeologists see in them great

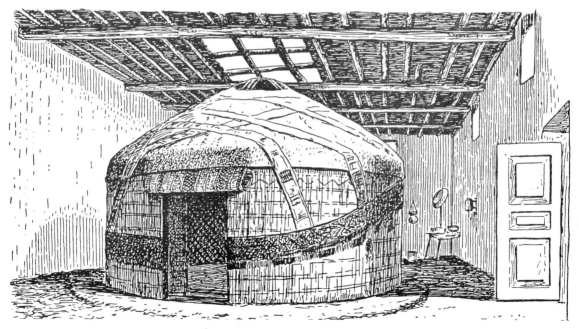

89  *Functional yurt in a modern building (1954) near the Aral Sea (Ždanko). The survival of ancient traditions of habitation has been frequently reported by Soviet ethnologists.*

*90   Below: Plan of the gorodišče of Bel'sk with its
ramparts stretching for 20.5 miles (33 km) (Šramko).*

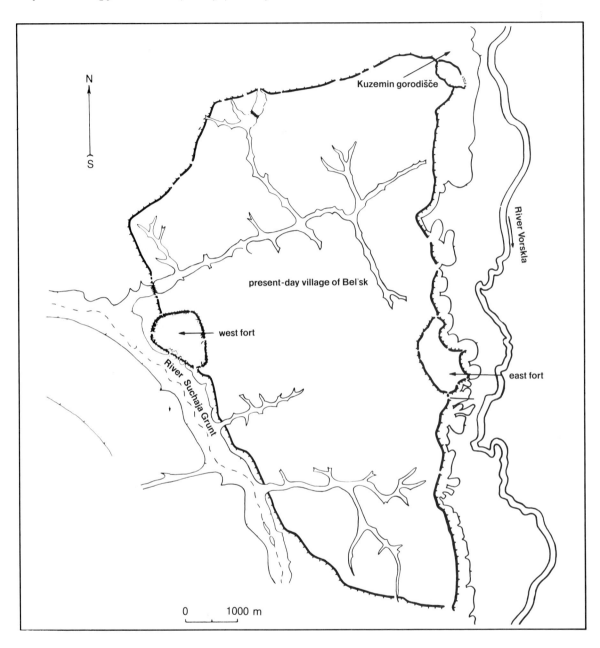

N
S

Kuzemin gorodišče

River Vorskla

present-day village of Bel'sk

west fort

River Suchaja Grunt

east fort

0   1000 m

tribal centres similar to the Celtic *oppida* in the west.

By far the most impressive fortified settlement in the forest steppe is the *gorodišče* of Bel'sk, which for some years has been the subject of intensive investigation by a team from the University of Khar'kov. It will certainly be decades before the necessary research is completed, but interim reports have already been published by B.N. Šramko, the director of the operation. The scale of the site is astonishing. The ramparts are 20.5 miles (33 km) in length, and in the form of an irregular triangle they enclose a plateau partitioned by stream courses and loess channels, linking three separate forts into one huge whole which has an area of approximately 4000 hectares. Two forts with their own ramparts, with areas of 72 and 62 hectares, lie in the west and the east of the site, both controlling wide river valleys. The Kuzemin *gorodišče* is just beyond the ramparts on the north-eastern side, part of a later phase of extension which was probably intended to protect an ancient harbour on the river Vorskla. The oldest building phase of the whole enclosure has so far been traced back to the seventh or sixth century, and it existed up to the third century BC. The greatest extension seems to have taken place during the second building phase, when, for instance, the ramparts surrounding the east fort reached a width of a good 59 ft (18 m) and were surmounted by a wooden wall at least 23 ft (7 m) high. The ditch around it is 20 ft (6 m) wide and deep. So far the amount of labour involved has only been calculated for the west fort: 11 million (human) working days.

Various types of dwelling, some built above ground with an area of roughly 1809 sq ft (170 sq m), some constructed in pits underground, characterize the inner building area of both the east and west forts, suggesting that there was a settled population. Pottery ovens, foundries and the like testify to a flourishing craft industry. Agriculture and livestock-rearing were well developed, and there is also evidence of horticultural activity. The contents of the granaries made possible the series of scientific observations mentioned

above in the section on cultivated plants.

It was assumed at first that the huge inner area surrounded by ramparts was used merely as protected pasture and as a pen. Meanwhile it has been established that at least a further nine areas within the inner plateau were inhabited – perhaps by tribes who for long periods of the year led a nomadic existence.

Several large cemeteries lie just beyond the ramparts. Even today over a thousand burial mounds can be seen outside the west fort, and in the last century there were far more. Places of sacrifice, deposits of grain and meat, and indications of human sacrifice are among the interesting finds. The first discovery of a 'skull-cup workshop' was also made here.

Šramko believes he has found in Bel'sk the ancient settlement of Gelonus, and a number of scholars agree with this. Before we can be certain either way, however, we must wait for future results from the excavations.

## The royal residence in the Kamenskoe *gorodišče*

In contrast to the forest steppe the steppe region to the south of it contains only one large site of this kind. This is the *gorodišče* of Kamenka (*Kamenskoe gorodišče* in Russian), a large fortified enclosure situated on the left bank of the Dnieper opposite Nikopol', 199 miles (320 km) from the river mouth. The steep banks of the Dnieper, and of the Konka and the Bol'saya Belozerka which both flow into the Dnieper at this point, were cleverly exploited in its construction. The ramparts of the fort were so conspicuous that they were mentioned in travel accounts as early as the sixteenth century. The first archaeological finds did not appear until the middle of the last century, however, and extensive excavations took place between 1937 and 1950 (interrupted during and immediately after the war), although considering the size of the site they have been on only a modest scale.

The Kamenskoe *gorodišče* has an area of 4.6 sq miles (12 sq km), of which 3.5 sq miles (9 sq km) consist of sand dunes by the name

91 *Plan of the Kamenskoe gorodišče (after Grakov):*

1 *Scythian settlement layer with metallurgical remains (c. 900 hectares in area)*
2 *Cemetery of flat graves*
3 *Pit house*
4 *Excavated burial mound*
5 *Unexcavated burial mound*
6 *Eighteenth-century ramparts*
7 *Scythian ramparts*
8 *Pre-Scythian settlement*

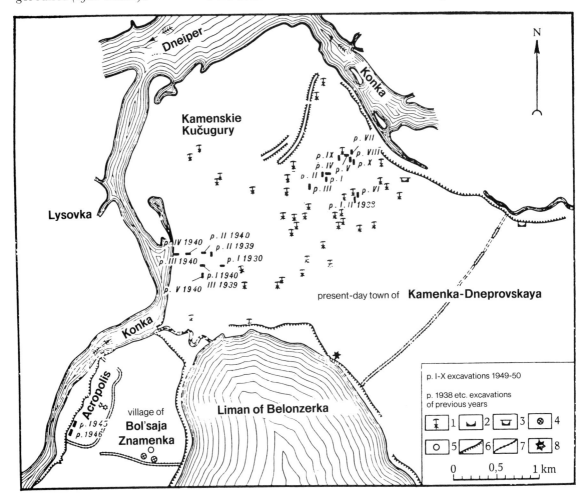

of *Kamenskie Kučugury.* The site divides into two complexes which are spatially clearly separated from each other: an 'acropolis' (or *kremlin*) in the south west, and the *Kučugury* where the ordinary people lived. In the south east and south west, where there are no steep river banks, kilometres of earth rampart close off the area from the open steppe.

As large sections of the *gorodišče* were flooded by the Kachovka reservoir, the excavations took on the character of an emergency salvage operation. Detailed investigations were undertaken of the living and working quarters of the craftsmen in the *Kučugury*, whereas the acropolis section was accorded only scant attention. It was the original intention to continue the excavations here, but unfortunately they have not been resumed, so that this part of the site remains virtually unexplored. There are practically no scientific analyses of the site; compared to the advanced investigative methods of the Bel'sk excavations, the Kamenskoe *gorodišče* has thus fallen far behind. The discoveries are sensational enough, however: a large specialist metal-working centre, and all the indications of a royal residence on the nearby acropolis. This 'fortress of metal-workers' is surrounded by a ring of open smallholding sites from the same period, usually no more than 0.5 to 1 hectare in size. These evidently served to provide agricultural produce for the craftsmen, for although there are definite signs of manufacturing activity and livestock-breeding in the *Kučugury* area, there is hardly any evidence of agriculture.

The outlines of numerous houses together with larger building complexes indicate a relative density of population in the inner section of the *Kučugury*. On the other hand there was a strip of land 2625–3937 ft (800–1200 m) wide between the south-east rampart and the actual inner area which remained empty and was only settled – if at all – in a kind of allotment system. Possibly it was used for keeping livestock. Within the inner section there are unusually clear traces of metal-working covering an area of almost 900 hectares. Nineteenth-century visitors were already wondering at the many heaps of slag and pieces of iron visible on the surface. Unfortunately no calculations have been made of the approximate extent of production. Considering the size of the area settled the excavations are very inadequate, and this together with the unsatisfactory evaluation of their finds does not allow any clear idea of the number of smelting furnaces operating at the same time, the approximate amount of iron produced or the number of foundries working alongside each other. Lumps of iron of relatively uniform weight and evidence of sawing indicate that they may have been processed into bars for trading purposes. The excavations unearthed the remains of smelting furnaces, pieces of ore, many lumps of iron, drops spilt during casting, fragments of crucibles and moulds, as well as numerous finished and half-finished products which provide an insight into the various stages of work and the range of goods produced. Here we have 'all round' metallurgists, who were involved in winning the metal and – especially in the case of iron – all the stages of production from extracting the ore to turning out the finished product. Forging was of course of the utmost importance, especially smithies producing battle equipment. Weapons, arm-our parts and horse-trappings were made here, the three essential components which, owing to constant wear in daily use and on campaigns, were needed in large quantities. We can assume that this was a great weapon-producing centre under direct royal supervision which also included gold- and silver-smiths' workshops.

The Kamenskoe *gorodišče* was geographically particularly well situated. For one thing it lay just below the Dnieper rapids which originally obstructed river traffic. The Greek town of Olbia was thus easily reached, which together with the local population was doubtless the main trading partner. In addition, the *gorodišče* lay right on a Dnieper ford which provided easy access to the west bank. Today, one of the largest iron-mining centres of the Soviet Union – the Krivoi Rog basin, with an excellent quality of ore of between 30 and 67 per cent iron content – is only 37 miles (60 km) away from here. In contrast to all the other iron deposits in the Ukraine, the ore here lies close to the surface and can in part even be quarried. After penetrating a relatively thin layer of loess, mining the ore in shafts and tunnels was not a particular problem even for the Scythians, especially as their skills in tomb-construction had provided them with an expertise in shifting earth. Traces of mining from Scythian times were discovered in places near the town of Krivoi Rog; the analysis of ore specimens from the Kamenskoe *gorodišče* has proved that they originated from this ancient mining region.

It was presumably owing to the lack of wood that ore had to be transported, and this would have been a further reason for choosing the Kamenskoe *gorodišče*. Apart from its proximity to iron ore deposits, the site on the banks of the Dnieper also afforded access to the extensive lowland forests. This made the transport of the large quantities of wood required for ore smelting much easier, since it could be floated down the Dnieper on rafts. Copper, lead and zinc were also smelted in addition to iron. There are zinc deposits in the nearby lower Dnieper region, but lead and copper had to be brought from a great distance.

From the point of view of fortification the acropolis stood in the most favourable position, at the top of the steep bank of the Dnieper where it reaches a height of 66 ft (20 m) (parts of it subsequently subsided). It was surrounded by ramparts, on top of which stood a wall constructed of air-dried bricks made of a special clay compound. Vestiges of a mysterious arrangement of columns were found along the top of the steep bank, the significance of which has not been established. The remains of houses with stone foundations were discovered in the inner area. As mentioned above, the acropolis was quite separate from the metal-working craft centre, and its layers did not reveal any remains indicating these activities. On the contrary, the inhabitants pursued quite different occupations: the proportion of the bones of wild game is higher in the acropolis than anywhere else in the whole of Scythia – more than 20 per cent (normally it was just 5 per cent). The large quantity of Greek pottery with painted red figures clearly indicates the wealth of the inhabitants, who were able to afford these costly imported objects. Drinking vessels and amphorae are further proof of the oft-quoted Scythian partiality for Greek wine.

From the time of the founding of the Kamenskoe *gorodišče* – the transition from the fifth to the fourth century BC – an impressive concentration of graves developed in its vicinity. It is similar to the Gerrhus grave landscape mentioned by Herodotus, and includes the graves of all the princes and kings of the time. Some of these, such as the Solocha kurgan, are so close to the *gorodišče* that we might be justified in assuming a direct connection. The importance of the Kamenskoe *gorodišče* is so apparent that it can hardly have been the seat of minor tribal aristocracy, but must have been a royal place of residence. Details of the building plan, the structure and organization of the whole complex and above all of which rulers resided in the 'acropolis' may best be established through further excavation.

Sites such as the Bel'sk and Kamenskoe *gorodišče*, to which further examples could be added, show clearly that town planning in Scythia was not merely a reflection of Mediterranean ideas, as was for a long time assumed. The extraordinarily spacious complexes with their 'acropolis' area seem to be orientated more towards Near Eastern models. The architecture too was not derived from Mediterranean forms: on the contrary, the robust building style which was adapted to climatic conditions influenced the Greeks, as shown in parts of Olbia, Berezan' and other Greek colonies. Archaeologists are faced with considerable difficulties regarding the interpretation of these sites which since the start of their systematic exploration have significantly contributed to the refinement of our picture of the Scythians.

# 8 The Scythian kings

## Social structure, religion and 'philosophy'

The Scythians attributed the origin of their kings to a mythical progenitor of divine descent by the name of Targitaus. Their Greek neighbours in the north Pontic cities also assigned a demigod to them as ancestor: had not Heracles reached the then uninhabited Scythian country in his wanderings, and been forced there to become the lover of a fabulous being, half woman and half serpent? This creature, who lived in a cave in the wooded district of Hylaea, is said to have borne him three sons, of whom only the youngest, Scythes, passed the test of strength in bending the bow, set by his father, thus becoming the ancestor of the royal Scythian kings. We are familiar with his pretty, 'serpent-footed' mother from several depictions; her 'descendants' adorned their horses' brows with her image in gold or silver.

As far as we can gather from written sources, three kings always ruled simultaneously in Scythia, of whom one was given the honour, function, and rank of 'king-in-chief', having his seat in the largest of the three kingdoms. We know relatively little of the social structure. Under the kings there were 'nomarchs' (evidently great land magnates); other Scythian ranks and classes mentioned are sceptre-bearers, 'the noble', 'the distinguished', spear-carriers, soothsayers, 'ordinary people' and slaves. The royal title was always hereditary; but we do not know the terms of inheritance in any detail, nor what conditions the prince had to fulfil in order to become king. That the succession could not always be settled conjointly is shown by the historically-documented fratricide in the family of King Ariapeithes.

## The King's signet ring

The confirmation of written sources through archaeological finds – even on only fragile evidence – often involves the rehabilitation of an ancient author whose reliability had previously not been too highly rated. The accounts given by Herodotus have also, as we have seen, been reinforced on many points by the results of modern research, becoming more colourful and vivid in the process. This applies also in the case of a find which came to light completely unexpectedly and which seems to confirm as a historical event one of the most dramatic episodes in Book IV of Herodotus.

In order to explain its importance, we have to immerse ourselves, with the help of the ancient account (Herodotus IV, 78–80), in the genealogy of the Scythian kings and the intrigue in the house of Ariapeithes which ended in fratricide. King Ariapeithes was king-in-chief of the Scythians around the time of Herodotus's visit to Olbia, and his agent Tymnes was Herodotus's source of information. Ariapeithes had three wives of different nationalities: a Greek from Istria in the south, a daughter of the Thracian King Teres (neither of their names is known) and a Scythian called Opoea. Each of these wives had a son; the son of the wife from Istria was called Scylas, that of the Thracian princess Octamasades, and the Scythian's son was called Oricus. After Ariapeithes had been murdered by Spargapeithes, King of the Agathyrsi, Scylas succeeded to the throne, acquiring at the same time also Opoea, one of the former wives of his father.

Scylas's mother had taught him to speak and write in Greek, and her education seems altogether to have alienated him from Scythian culture. The King found himself discon-

123

92 Left: Golden dish with raised centre (Omphalus dish), according to Herodotus a typical symbol of the Scythian kings which they wore on their belts. From the Kul'-Oba kurgan (Photo: Marburg).

93 The 'serpent-footed' goddess, according to legend the progenitrix of the Scythian kings. Horse's gold face ornament from the Cimbalka kurgan.

tented with the Scythian way of life and grew more and more fond of Olbia, where he had a large, costly palace built surrounded by griffons and sphinxes of white marble. Whenever he went to the town with his army he would leave his men outside the walls and enter alone, without a bodyguard or the usual escort. Once inside he would change into Greek clothing and live according to Greek custom – often for a month or even longer. He also married a Greek woman from the town and sacrificed to Greek gods – all of this secretly, of course. He had the gates of the fortified town locked and guarded so that no Scythian could observe his activities.

It was during his initiation into the secret cult of Bacchic Dionysus, a cult bound up with ecstatic excesses where the participants were overcome with a 'divine madness', that events began to escalate. His palace in the town was struck by lightning and burnt to the ground, and the Scythians learnt of the strange activities of their ruler. Since the adoption of alien and in particular Greek customs was abhorred in Scythia, the chief Scythians present outside the town had themselves led secretly up a tower from where they saw the King with their own eyes as he went past, presumably in an advanced stage of Dionysiac madness and in undignified garb. Scylas was deposed, and while his half-brother Octamasades was being chosen as the new king he fled to Thrace, probably in order to reach his mother's home town from there.

The new King set out in pursuit of his fleeing brother and reached the Danube with his army. There, on the border, the Thracian army with his uncle at the head drew up opposite him, but at the last minute at the Thracians' suggestion the two leaders came to an agreement: there was to be a mutual exchange of unpopular relations who had each sought refuge with the other side. Sitalces, the Thracian king, was given his brother who had fled to the Scythians, and the hapless Scylas was delivered into the hands of Octamasades who, it is said, beheaded him on the spot.

This fraternal feud in the Scythian royal household and its attendant circumstances, reminiscent of the bloody dynastic struggles

of medieval times, are known to us only through Herodotus. It would seem therefore that scepticism at the very least would in this case be appropriate. So far it has not been possible to identify for certain any of the rich royal burials as that of one of the Scythian kings known to us by name. Specific costly objects with a name on, which would enable us to classify them with certainty, are almost totally lacking. In the case of those we do have, the name has no connection with any historical information, and we are still left groping in the dark.

All the more exciting, therefore, was the discovery of a heavy gold signet ring engraved with the Greek inscription SKYLEO and the depiction of a figure on a chair or throne, probably a Scythian goddess. Scylas's signet

94 *The Istria signet ring with the inscription SKYLEO = property of Scylas.*

ring was found only 6 miles (10 km) from Istria, not far from the Danube – almost exactly where the events described above are said to have taken place. A signet ring is a very personal object: even in Scythian times such rings were unique, and this one differs sharply from all the others in our possession through the unusual circumstance of the name-engraving and also in the nature of the depiction.

Did Scylas hand over the ring to someone else? Was it lost during his flight, or stolen from the dead man? Or was it taken from the unrecognized and looted grave of the fugitive King who, torn between two opposing cultures, had come to such an unhappy end? We do not know. The search for the remains of his magnificent palace during excavations in Olbia has up to now also been unsuccessful, although such an exceptional building would be immediately noticeable among the otherwise simple town dwellings, even where all lie in ruins. Further excavations may perhaps answer some of these questions at a future date.

## Rex Scytharum Atheas

Probably the most original figure among the Scythian kings was Ateas, who fell in battle against Philip II of Macedonia in the early summer of 339 BC. Greek sources refer to him as *Basileus Skython Ateas*, and in Latin sources he is known as *Rex Scytharum*, and Strabo gives the additional information that he ruled over the mass of barbarians in the region north of the Black Sea. There are many references to this king in ancient literature, and if they are taken together it becomes apparent that relatively few items of information are repeated. New episodes and anecdotes are continually offered which are not stereotyped; they all appear to be original, and serve to characterize Ateas as a Scythian *par excellence*.

He preferred the neighing of his horses to the warbling of flutes, it was reported – doubtless with horror, for he had made this remark after a concert given by the most celebrated Greek flautist, who had been taken prisoner. Philip's emissaries described on their return from Scythia how Ateas had given them an audience while he was grooming his horse, and had even asked affably whether their ruler did the same.

In a threatening letter to the inhabitants of Byzantium he told them that they had better not try to frustrate his plans, otherwise his mares would drink their water.

Philip II, intending to appoint himself the 90-year-old's heir, found himself cheated of his wish and humiliated by Ateas's message that he had a son of his own. In order to camouflage his invasion of a foreign land, Philip announced that he was only intending to put up a statue of Heracles at the mouth of the Danube. But Ateas saw through the trick and replied that the statue should be handed over to him and he would see that it was erected and given due respect. He could, however, on no account agree to foreign troops marching through his territory, and the setting up of the said statue against his, Ateas's will was also out of the question. If this should be attempted, he added, his warriors would make bronze arrowheads from the statue. It was no wonder that the Macedonian King, highly provoked, spared no pains to destroy this adversary. Of the battle itself we know only that Philip positioned his best riders to the rear of the warriors, with orders to kill anyone trying to flee.

The historical status of Ateas is disputed. From some sides he is seen only as a minor western king who in his expansion westwards came into conflict with Philip II. The history of the period leading up to the war with Philip is confusing and does not help to clarify matters. Another view is that Ateas was the central king who united the whole of Scythia for the first time under one rule. (Whether he was an earlier 'king-in-chief' with two kings subordinate to him is similarly not clear from the sources.) The majority of Soviet experts support the second theory, and with good reason. Bearing in mind that Ateas – if he did in fact reach such a biblical age – must have been born around 430 BC, and considering the nature of the following period, as revealed through archaeology, we can form a fairly clear picture of the situation. The fourth century, the time of Ateas's reign, is considered to be Scythia's 'golden age' and characterized by the building of extravagant settlement complexes like the Kamenskoe *gorodišče*, and by the great burial landscape in the Dnieper bend district where the graves of princes and kings show evidence of immense riches and power. Against this background it is difficult to imagine any decentralization, or indeed incursions to the west on the part of a relatively unimportant minor king; it seems more likely to have been the political design of a central power. The fact that Ateas was still leading his army personally into battle also reinforces the idea that as a symbolic figure he must have been far more high-ranking than a minor king.

The conflict with Philip cost Ateas his life, but his adversary, who was similarly advanced in years, did not gain any real advantage from his victory. Philip was seriously injured in the campaign – a lance pierced his thigh with such force that his horse was killed under him by the thrust. And in addition his Scythian booty was taken back from him by recalcitrant tribes.

Coins also contribute to the Ateas question – five finds have been reported so far in scholarly literature. They bear the name of the king, and depict a typical Scythian rider with drawn bow, possibly an attempt to represent the ageing ruler in person.

The Scythian pantheon was fairly extensive. Apart from the main goddess Tabiti, goddess of the hearth, we know of a series of deities whose rank order and areas of responsibility have only come down to us in Greek translation. According to this, the Scythian gods were as follows: Papeaus (equivalent to Zeus) and Api (his wife), Oetosyrus (the Scythian

95  *One of the five extant coins of King Ateas (ATAIAS) (Photo: Anochin).*

128

Apollo), Argimpasa (Celestial Aphrodite), Thagimasadas (a 'Poseidon'), Heracles, and a god of war or the sword to whom great sacrificial mounds were raised and over whose emblem, an ancient iron sword, the blood of animals and human beings was poured.

The King was surrounded by a large number of soothsayers, who practised their divinations using willow rods and the inner bark of the lime-tree. If their soothsaying was shown to be flawed their punishment was death by burning.

## Anacharsis, the wise man from the steppe

To conclude our account of the Scythian world we shall briefly consider its underlying philosophical ideas, of which we have only a fragmentary knowledge.

In harmony with their nature-orientated way of life and animal style in art, the Scythians' philosophy, as represented by Anacharsis, was also very closely related to nature. This Scythian philosopher became so celebrated in Greece that he was even included among the Seven Sages. It seems that he went to Athens in 590 BC, there becoming the friend of Solon, with whom he debated. The philosopher from afar was of royal lineage, possibly the brother of the reigning Scythian king, and it was presumably by reason of his noble birth that he was granted Attic citizenship and admitted to the Eleusinian Mysteries, an honour otherwise denied to barbarians. His extensive knowledge and his wisdom earned him admiration on all sides, especially after his participation in a 'wisdom competition'. On his return to his homeland, he is said to have met his death at the hands of his brother when he was caught practising the cult of Cybele and accused of having adopted foreign religious customs.

The figure of Anacharsis and his tragic death made a strong impression on his contemporaries and on later authors, and many references to him and reports of his sayings are found in the literature of antiquity. We shall conclude our brief summary of the culture of this extinct horse-riding people with an episode surviving in the fragments from the ninth book of Diodorus (Vales. Excerpt S.23) which reveals something of the Scythian mind:

Croesus sent for those men of Greece most renowned for their wisdom, and showing them the immense wealth of his treasuries, he bestowed rich gifts on those who praised his good fortune. And just as he had summoned to him those whose wisdom was most celebrated he also sent for Solon, for he intended that the testimony of these men should confirm his great happiness. Thus Anacharsis the Scythian, and Bias and Solon and Pittaeus came to him and were all honoured and feasted together. He showed his riches and the greatness of his power to them also. At that time, however, men of learning were concise in their style of speech. Now when Croesus had shown these men the splendour of his realm and the great numbers of those who served him, he asked Anacharsis, the oldest among the wise men, which living being on earth he considered the bravest. Anacharsis said: the wildest animals, for they alone died willingly for their freedom. Croesus thought that this was the wrong answer but believed that the answer to his second question would be according to his wish, and so he asked him whom he considered to be the most righteous. But Anacharsis answered again: the wildest animals, for they alone lived according to nature and not according to laws; and whereas nature was the work of God, the law was only the invention of man, and surely it was more just to abide by the works of God than by those of man. And now, wishing to get the better of Anacharsis, Croesus asked him whether he thought the wildest animals also the wisest: but the other declared this at once to be true, explaining that it was indeed a mark of wisdom to set the truth of nature above the statutes of the law. Croesus however ridiculed him, as if these answers savoured of Scythia and a bestial way of life.

96, 97  *Burial of a late Scythian king from the mausoleum of the city of Neapolis Scythica in the Crimea, which superseded the Kamenskoe gorodišče centre. The mausoleum contained 72 rich burials, of which the one illustrated here attracted particular interest owing to its grave layout and its opulence. The inventory includes weapons, jewellery and typical articles of clothing, which can be dated back to the second century BC. The excavator P. N. Šul'c produced a reconstruction of the archaeological find (see opposite).*

The burial is probably that of King Scilurus, who is documented in written sources, or of his eldest son Palacus who ruled after him. Ancient legend attributes 50 or even 80 sons to Scilurus, and he is said to have summoned them to him when he realized his end was near. He caused each one to break a javelin, a task they all managed easily. Scilurus then took 80 javelins and commanded each to break the whole sheaf, which proved impossible. After this symbolic act the old king cautioned his sons that they could only be strong and invincible if they were united, while the individual would be easily destroyed.

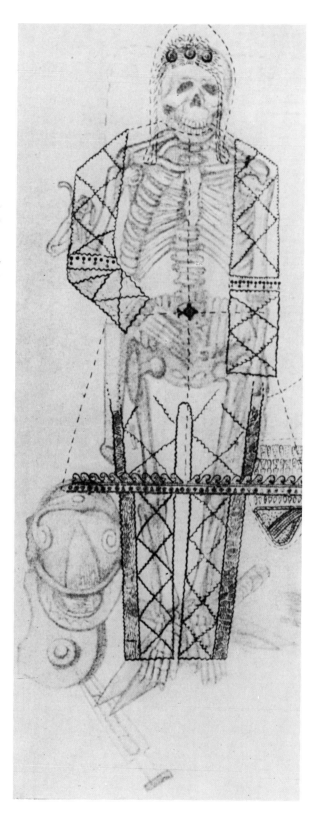

# Historical summary

| | |
|---|---|
| Eighth century BC | Land acquisition in region north of the Black Sea. Scythians invading from the east drive out Cimmerians who had settled there. |
| Seventh – sixth century BC | Scythian campaigns into and apparent 28-year domination of the Near East.<br>Scythian (?) King Partatua demands one of the daughters of the Assyrian king Asarhaddon in marriage.<br>The Caucasus becomes the 'Scythian route' to the south. |
| c. 592 BC | The Scythian philosopher Anacharsis in Athens (as Solon's contemporary and debating partner). He is later chosen as one of the Seven Sages of Greece. |
| c. 585 BC | Scythians play a decisive part in the destruction of the ancient Artaic empire in Transcaucasia. |
| 520/19 BC | The Persian king Darius's campaign against the Asiatic Scythians. Skuka, king of the Sakas 'of the pointed helmets', is defeated and taken prisoner. |
| 513/12 BC | Darius's campaign against the European Scythians. 'King-in-chief' Idanthyrsus and the two subordinate Kings Taxakis and Skopasis put the Persian army to flight. |
| End of sixth – fifth century BC | Scythians recruited as police troops in Athens. |
| c. 510 BC | Scythian envoys attempt to arrange a military allegiance with Cleomenes, King of Sparta, against the Persians. |

| | |
|---|---|
| c. 450 BC | Herodotus visits Olbia and its environs. His Book IV describes the Scythians and their neighbours. |
| Second half of the fifth century BC | Founding of the fortification known today as the Kamenskoe *gorodišče*. During the ensuing period it develops into a complex resembling a town, with a metal-working centre and a royal residence. |
| Fourth century BC | Scythia's 'Golden Age'. Development of a burial landscape near the Dnieper rapids, with a concentration of royal graves. Dobruja ('Scythia Minor') brought under Scythian domination. |
| 339 BC | King Ateas, aged 90, killed in battle against Philip II of Macedonia, near the Danube. |
| 331 BC | Campaign of Zopyrion (Alexander the Great's governor in Thrace). Unsuccessful siege of Olbia, followed by complete annihilation of the army by the Scythians. |
| From third century BC | The Sarmatians advancing from the east gradually drive the Scythians back to the coastal areas and the Crimea. |
| End of third–beginning of second century BC | Scythian(?) King Saitapharnes threatens Olbia and is propitiated with gifts. |
| Second century BC | The newly-founded capital Neapolis Scythica (near Simferopol' in the Crimea) supersedes Kamenskoe *gorodišče*. King Scilurus and his family are interred in the mausoleum at the city wall. |
| 110 and 107 BC | King Palacus, son of Scilurus, suffers defeats at the hands of Diophantes, a commander of Mithradates VI of Pontus. |

| From AD 9 | Ovid, in exile in Tomis (modern Constanta in Rumania) on the western border of Scythia, calls the Black Sea the 'Scythian Sea' and tells of Scythian military operations. |
| First century AD | Continuation of a late Scythian culture, especially in the Crimea. |
| Third century AD | Destruction of Neapolis Scythica (possibly by Ostrogoths) and extinction of late Scythian culture. |

# Notes and references

1 'What an appalling sight! They are doing this themselves! So many palaces! What extraordinary strength of mind! What men! These are Scythians!' Quoted here from P.P. Comte de Ségur, *Histoire de Napoléon et de la Grande Armée pendant l'année 1812*, vol. 2, p. 54.

2 There is, however, scant awareness of other aspects of the culture of this independent group of mounted warriors on the Black Sea. It is not uncommon to meet with the prejudiced view that we cannot expect such a thing as 'culture' from nomads.

3 'I who was born to peaceful leisure far from the hurly-burly and led a soft and comfortable life shunning all hardship, now suffer exceedingly', was his lament. He was torn between a fear of death (imagining himself with horror having to wander as a lonely Roman shade among those of savages) and a longing for death (which led him to compose his own epitaph). In desperation he even tried his hand at writing in a foreign language, regarding himself as 'almost a Getian poet' ('Oh the shame! I have even written poetry in the Getian language'), although Thracian grated on his ears.

4 'Tristia per vacuos horrent absinthia campos' (Ovid, *Epistulae ex Ponto* III, 1, 14).

5 Ilya Repin (1844–1930): *The Zaporozhye Cossacks writing a letter to Sultan Muhamed IV, 1891*, Russian Museum, Leningrad.

6 Quotation translated from *Wilhelm von Rubruk, Reise zu den Mongolen 1253–1255* ('Journey to the Mongols'), translated and edited with notes by F. Risch, Leipzig 1934, p. 34.

7 Quotation translated from H. Otten, *Hethitische Totenrituale* ('Hittite funeral rites'), German Academy of Science, Berlin, Institute of Oriental Studies, Publication No. 37, 1958, p. 42.

8 Ovid, *Tristia* V, 10.

9 For this information I am indebted to the forensic doctor Steffen Berg (Göttingen), who kindly agreed to make a theoretical assessment of the possible toxic effects of the poison.

10 *Nagaica* = cat-o'-nine-tails.

11 (Translated) quotation from the journal of the 'Master of Ceremonies of the Great Gate', ed. R.F. Kreutel. Dtv Dokumente No. 450, 1976, p. 32.

12 (Translated) quotation from J.G. Kohl, *Reisen in Südrußland*, ('Journeys through southern Russia'), Part 1, 1841, p. 24; Part 2, 1841, p. 234.

13 Herodotus IV, 66.

14 It has been suggested that the fact that women were armed was due to both a 'need for assertion' and, against the background of a general increase in military involvement, a kind of 'young girls' sport before marriage' which was retained by some women well into maturity. The theory has also been put forward that the Amazons constituted a special group in society, perhaps even a particularly 'emancipated' one, or that they were a relic of an earlier matriarchal society.

15 An Islamic secret society (c.1100–1200 BC) whose members used hashish to work themselves into a trance before going into battle.

16 Kohl, 1841, p. 181.

17 Kohl, 1841, p. 194.

# Select bibliography

## General

M.I. Artamonov, *Goldschatz der Skythen in der Eremitage*, Prague 1970.

G. Charrière, *L'art barbare scythe*, Paris 1971.

A.M. Chazanov, *Zoloto skifov* (Scythian Gold), Moscow 1975.

M. Ebert, *Südrußland im Altertum*, Bonn 1921.

L.A. El'nickijj, *Skifija evrazijskich stepej*, Novosibirsk 1977.

B.N. Grakow, *Die Skythen*, Berlin 1978.

F. Hančar, *Die Skythen als Forschungsproblem*, Reinecke-Festschrift, Mainz 1950, pp. 67–83.

V.A. Il'inskaja, *Skify dneprovskogo lesostepnogo levoberež'ja*, Kiev 1968.

---, *Ranneskifskie kurgany bassejna r. Tjasmin*, Kiev 1975.

K. Jettmar, *Die frühen Steppenvölker*, Kunst der Welt, Baden-Baden 1964.

A.M. Leskov, *Treasures from the Ukrainian barrows: latest discoveries*, Leningrad 1972.

E.H. Minns, *Scythians and Greeks*, Cambridge 1913.

H. Portratz, *Die Skythen in Südrußland*, Basle 1963.

M. Rostowzew, *Skythien und der Bosporus*, vol. 1, Berlin 1931.

B.A. Rybakov, *Gerodotova Skifija*, Moscow 1979.

A.P. Smirnow, *Die Skythen*, Dresden 1979.

T. Talbot Rice, *The Scythians*, London 1957.

F. Trippett, *The First Horsemen*, New York 1974.

J. Wiesner, *Die Kulturen der frühen Reitervölker*, Handbuch der Kulturgeschichte, Frankfurt 1968 (new edition: *Studienausgaben zur Kulturgeschichte*, Frankfurt 1973).

A survey of the most important finds is contained in the catalogues of the main exhibitions in France and the USA: *From the Lands of the Scythians. Ancient Treasures from the Museum of the USSR*, The Metropolitan Museum of Art, The Los Angeles County Museum of Art (o. J.). *Or des Scythes. Trésors des musées soviétiques*, Paris 1975.

Information on the latest research can be found in the following journals:
*Skifskie drevnosti* (Scythian antiquities). Kiev 1973.
*Skifskij mir* (Scythian world). Kiev 1975.
*Skify i sarmaty* (Scythians and Sarmatians). Kiev 1977.
*Skify i Kavkaz* (Scythians and the Caucasus). Kiev 1980.

## The land of the Scythians

V.F. Gajdukevič, *Das Bosporanische Reich*, 2nd ed., Berlin 1971.

J.G. Kohl, *Reisen in Südrußland*, Parts 1 and 2, Dresden and Leipzig 1841.

K. Neumann, *Die Hellenen im Skythenlande*, Berlin 1855.

Publius Ovidius Naso, *Tristia epistulas ex Ponto* (Letters written in exile).

E. Roesler, *Die Geten und ihre Nachbarn*, Sitzungsberichte der philosophisch-historischen Classe der Kaiserlichen Akademie der Wissenschaften, vol. 44, Vienna 1863, pp. 140–87.

W. von Rubruk, *Reise zu den Mongolen 1253 bis 1255*.

# Death and burial

*Antiquités du Bosphore cimmérien*, St Petersburg 1854.

A.A. Bobrinskoi, *Kurgany i slučvajnye archeologičeskie nachodki bliz mestečka Smely*, vol. I–III, St Petersburg 1887–1901.

*Drevnosti Gerodotovoi Skifii*, 2 vols., St Petersburg 1866–1872.

A. Leskov, 'Die skythischen Kurgane', *Antike Welt, Zeitschrift für Archäologie und Urgeschichte*, 1974 (special issue).

B.N. Mozolevski, *Tovsta mogila*, Kiev 1979.

K. Ranke, *Indogermanische Totenverehrung*, vol. 1, Der dreißigste und vierzigste Tag im Totenkult der Indogermanen, FF Communications No. 140, Helsinki 1951.

R. Rolle, *Totenkult der Skythen*. Part I, Das Steppengebiet, Vorgeschichtliche Forschungen, vol. 18, Berlin and New York 1979.

S.I. Rudenko, *Frozen Tombs of Siberia*, London 1970.


# Other tribes inhabiting the region north of the Black Sea

**Cimmerians:**
A.I. Terenožkin, *Kimmerijcy*, Kiev 1976.
**Sauromatians:**
K.F. Smirnov, *Savromaty*, Moscow 1964.
**Tauri:**
A.M. Leskov, *Gornyj Krim v pervom tysjačeletii do našej ery*, Kiev 1965.
**Sindi and Maeotae:**
N.V. Anfimov, *Iz prošlogo Kubani*, Krasnodar 1958.
**Thracians:**
I. Venedikov, T. Gerassimov, *Thrakische Kunst*, Leipzig 1976.
A.I. Meljukova, *Skifija i frakijskij mir*, Moscow 1979.


# At the eastern end of the Scythian world

K.A. Akišev, *Kurgan Issyk* (Issyk mound. The Art of Saka in Kazakhstan), Moscow 1978.

M.I. Artamonov, *Sokrovišča sakov, Pamjatniki drevnego iskusstva*, Moscow 1973.

M.P. Griaznov, M.Ch. Mannai-ool, *Kurgan Aržan* (forthcoming).

M. Griasnow, 'Südsibirien', *Archaeologia mundi*, Stuttgart, Munich, Geneva, Paris 1970.


# Weapons and fighting methods

E.V. Cernenko, *Skifskij dospech*, Kiev 1968.

A.M. Chazanov, *Očerki voennogo dela sarmatov*, Moscow 1971.

W. Ginters, *Das Schwert der Skythen und Sarmaten in Südrußland*, Berlin 1928.

A. Hančar, 'Die Bogenwaffe der Skythen', *Mitteilungen der Anthropologischen Gesellschaft in Wien*, vol. 102, 1973, pp. 3–25.

A.I. Meljukova, 'Vooruženie skifov', *Svod archaeologičeskich istočnikov* D 1–4, Moscow 1964.

W. Rätzel, 'Die skythischen Gorytbeschläge', *Bonner Jahrbücher*, vol. 178, 1978, pp. 163–80.

R. Rolle, *Oiorpata*. Materialhefte zur Ur- und Frühgeschichte Niedersachsens, vol. 17 (festschrift for K. Raddatz), 1980.

H.-J. Schnitzler, 'Der Sakenfeldzug Dareios' des Großen', *Antike und Universalgeschichte*, Münster 1972, pp. 52–71.

E. von Stern, *Der Pfeilschuß des Olbiopoliten Anaxagoras*, annual report of the Austrian Archaeological Institute in Vienna, vol. 4, No. 2, 1901, pp. 57–9 and supplement, pp. 61–70.

V.V. Struve, *Pochod Darija I na sakov-massagetov*, Izvestija Akademii nauk SSSR, serija istorii i filosofii No. 3, 1946, pp. 231–50.


# Episodes from everyday Scythian life

O.D. Ganina, *Antični bronzy z Piščanogo* (The Ancient Bronzes of Peščanoe), Kiev 1970.

F. Hančar, ' 'Altai-Skythen' und Schamanismus', Actes du IV Congrès international des sciences anthropologiques et ethnologiques, Vienna 1952, tome III (publié 1956), pp. 183–9.

K. Meuli, 'Scythica', *Hermes*, Zeitschrift für klassische Philologie, vol. 70, Berlin 1935, pp. 121–76.

G. Ränk, *Skythisches Räucherwerk*, festschrift for Matthias Zender, Bonn 1972, pp. 490–96.

F. Hančar, 'Bauweise und Teppichkunst der eurasischen Reiternomaden in den Jahrhunderten um Christi Geburt', Mitteilungen der österreichischen Arbeitsgemeinschaft für Ur- und Frühgeschichte, vol. 20, Nos 1/6, Vienna 1969.

K. Jettmar, 'Zum 'Spielteppich' aus dem V. Pazyryk-Kurgan', *Central Asiatic Journal*, vol. 8, 1963, pp. 47–53.

S.I. Rudenko, *Drevnejšie v mire chudožestvennye kovry i tkani*, Moscow 1968.

C. Strauß, 'Musikinstrumente bei Reiternomaden Eurasiens', *Prähistorische Zeitschrift* (forthcoming).

v.u.Z.', *Slovenská archeologia* XXI–I, 1973, pp. 147–66.

W. Vogel, 'Pflugbau-Skythen und Hackbau-Skythen', Studien und Forschungen zur Menschen und Völkerkunde, vol. 14 (festschrift Ed. Hahn for his 60th birthday), Stuttgart 1917, pp. 150–66.

**On the Kamenskoe gorodišče:**

B.N. Grakov, 'Kamenskoe gorodišče', Materialy i issledovanija po archeologii SSSR, vol. 36, Moscow 1954.

**On Bel'sk:**

B.A. Šramko, 'Krepost'skifskoj epochi u s. Bel'sk – gorod Gelon'. *Skifksij mir*. Kiev 1975, pp. 94–132.

V.A. Il'inskaja, 'Možet li Bel'skoe gorodišče byt' gorodom Gelonom'. *Skify i sarmaty, Kiev 1977, pp. 73–95.*

**On Neapolis scythica** (late Scythian capital in the Crimea):

P. Šul'c, *Mavzolej Neapolja skifskogo*, Moscow 1953.

T. Vysockaja, *Skifskie gorodišče*, Simferopol' 1975.

# Animal husbandry, household and settlement

V.I. Calkin, 'Domašnie i dikie životnye severnogo Pričernomor'ja v epochu rannego železa', Materialy i issledovanija po archeologii SSSR, vol. 53, 1960, pp. 7–109.

F. Hančar, 'Der 'goldene Pflug' der skythischen Abstammungslegende in archäologischer Sicht', *Innsbrucker Beiträge zur Kulturwissenschaft*, vol. 14, 1968, pp. 307–23.

F. Hančar, 'Das Pferd in prähistorischer und früher historischer Zeit', *Wiener Beiträge zur Kulturgeschichte und Linguistik*, vol. 11, 1955.

R. Rolle, 'Rote Pferde – goldene Reiter, Betrachtungen zu den Pferden der Skythen', festschrift for R. Pittioni, Vienna 1976, pp. 756–76.

B.A. Šramko, 'Der Ackerbau bei den Stämmen Skythiens im 7.–3. Jahrhundert

# Social structure and religion

A.M. Chazanov, *Social'naja istorija skifov*, Moscow 1975.

D.S. Raevskij, *Očerki ideologii skifo-sakskich plemen*, Moscow 1977.

A.I. Terenožkin, 'Obščestvennyj stroj skifov', *Skify i sarmaty*, Kiev 1977, pp. 3–28.

# Scythian kings

V.A. Anochin, 'Monety Ateja', *Skifskie drevnosti*, Kiev 1973, pp. 20–41.

I.V. Brašinskij, *Sokrovišča skifskich carej*, Moscow 1967.

H.-J. Diesner, *Die Skythenkönige bei Herodot, Griechische Städte und einheimische Völker des Schwarzmeergebietes*, Berlin 1961, pp. 11–19.

D.V. Šelov, *Car' Atej*, Numizmatika i sfragistika, vol. 2, Kiev 1965, pp. 16–40.

# Index